Slim & Healthy RECIPES

CONTENTS

BEST OF FAVORITE RECIPES MAGAZINE
April 1988

Best of Favorite Recipes Magazine is published 4 times a year, quarterly, by Publications International, Ltd., 7373 N. Cicero Avenue, Lincolnwood, IL 60646. Manufactured in the USA.

On the front cover: Pacific Veal on Skewers (top left), Refrigerator Cheesecake with Raw Fruit Glaze (bottom right), Mushroom Vinaigrette Salad (bottom left).
On the back cover: Strawberry Ice Milk (top), Lime Sherbet (bottom).

COOKING THE
Slim & Healthy
WAY

The secrets for a stay-slender, stay-healthy life-style are simple: cut out unnecessary calories, avoid foods laden with fat and watch for excessive sodium and cholesterol. Also, develop some form of routine exercise program that you will enjoy, whether it be walking a short distance every day or swimming 20 miles a week.

The 1980s have been described as the decade of health, fitness and diet-consciousness. Shoppers now pay as much attention to the information on food labels as they do to the price, realizing that "you are what you eat." This cookbook can become part of a stay-slender, stay-healthy program. The recipes are low in calories, fat, cholesterol and sodium, and their ease of preparation is designed for today's busy and hectic schedules.

What Fat Is and How to Recognize It

Grab the loose flesh around your waist—that's one way to recognize fat. Another is to examine the calories in your diet. Calories are simply the measurement of the amount of energy the body can extract from any particular food. The body uses this food energy as fuel for its activities. Overweight is usually caused by taking in more food energy (calories) than the body uses. These excess calories are stored as body fat.

Fat, protein and carbohydrate (the three basic food elements) generate calories. Fatty foods are the biggest problem for the weight-conscious; a gram of fat contains more than twice as many calories (nine per gram) as an equal amount of either protein or carbohydrate (four per gram). Fat can be either animal or vegetable, but regardless of the source, the calories are the same. So every time you trim the fat off a steak or skim the grease from gravy or chicken stock, think of it as trimming the fat right off your own hips or waistline.

Cholesterol and Fat

Cholesterol is both manufactured by the body itself and absorbed into the body from foods of animal origin, such as egg yolks (more than 200 milligrams of cholesterol each), meats and dairy products. Some cholesterol is essential for normal body function. However, an excessive amount of cholesterol in the blood has been linked to coronary heart disease. Cholesterol levels in the blood are affected not only by foods that contain cholesterol directly, but also by the types of *fat* in foods.

Dietary fat comes in three forms: saturated, polyunsaturated and monounsaturated. Saturated fats are believed to be the villains that can increase blood cholesterol. These fats are usually solid at room temperature and include all forms of animal fat, such as butter, the fat in milk, cream and cheese, lard, and the fat encasing and marbled through meat. Poultry and fish contain less saturated fat per ounce than meat, and the fat itself is less saturated. Some vegetable fats, such as coconut and palm oils, cocoa butter and hydrogenated vegetable fats (solid shortening), are also highly saturated.

Polyunsaturated fats seem to lower blood cholesterol. These are usually liquid vegetable oils; they include safflower (the highest in polyunsaturated fat), sunflower, corn, cottonseed and soybean oils. Monounsaturated fats, such as olive and peanut oils, may also lower blood cholesterol, but not to the same degree as the polyunsaturates.

The message is this: less total fat means fewer calories, and less cholesterol and saturated fat may mean a healthier heart. The Departments of Agriculture and of Health and Human Services reflect this healthful advice in their dietary guidelines: (1)Eat a variety of foods. (2)Maintain ideal weight. (3)Avoid too much fat, saturated fat and cholesterol. (4)Eat foods with adequate fiber and starch. (5)Avoid too much sugar. (6)Avoid too much sodium. (7)If you drink alcohol, do so in moderation.

Sodium

About 17 percent of the American adult population has high blood pressure, which is thought to be related, in part, to excessive sodium in the diet. The National Research Council suggests the average healthy adult should limit consumption to 1,100 to 3,300 milligrams of sodium daily, yet the average intake is about 5,000 milligrams. Table salt, which is about 40 percent sodium, is the major source. A level teaspoon contains more than 2,000 milligrams of sodium. But remember, sodium can also be hidden. It occurs naturally in foods and is used as a flavoring agent or preservative in processed foods. So hold back on the salt shaker, when you cook and at the table, and read food package labels carefully.

Fiber

Fiber—or roughage—is the indigestible component found in fruits and vegetables, seeds, nuts and whole grains. Fiber contains no vitamins or minerals, no protein or fat and no calories. Then what good is it? Fiber does fill you up, helping to satisfy the appetite. One hundred calories worth of steak or cake may barely squelch your hunger pangs, but 100 calories of salad will probably do the job. In addition, fiber can help maintain the normal functioning of the body's intestinal system.

When introducing fiber into your diet, choose foods that are high in fiber but low in calories. Better to have 1 cup of lightly cooked green beans than 16 Brazil nuts. Both contain 2 grams of fiber, but the beans generate 50 calories, while the nuts, because of their high fat content generate 650 calories.

Be a Smart Shopper

The fight against excess fat in the kitchen really begins at the store. If you lose the first skirmish in the grocery aisle or at the meat counter, it could very well mean losing the whole battle. If you're a bargain hunter by instinct, you're used to reading labels, comparing packages and prices, to figure out which items are the best buys for the money. It's easy to apply those same skills and become a calorie-comparison shopper.

First, look for the nutrition information panel on the food package—but be aware you may not always find one. The Food and Drug Administration requires nutrition information panels only on "enriched" or "fortified" foods or on products that make nutritional claims, such as "low sodium" or "high in polyunsaturated fats." Many food manufacturers, however, are now voluntarily listing nutrition information.

Listed will be the percentage of the U.S. Recommended Daily Allowance (U.S. RDA) for protein and specific vitamins and minerals contained in the food. Recommended allowances are somewhat flexible, so the average healthy person does not need to consume exactly 100 percent of each nutrient each day. Soon, sodium may be listed on all food products displaying a nutrition information panel. At present, if sodium claims are made on the label, the product must meet certain standards set by the Food and Drug Administration. "Sodium-free" means the product must contain less than 5 milligrams of sodium per serving; "very low sodium" no more than 35 milligrams per serving; and "low sodium" no more than 140 milligrams per serving. "Reduced sodium," "unsalted" and "no-salt-added" usually indicate levels of sodium lower than in other comparable products. But remember that sodium does occur naturally in foods; "unsalted" or "no-salt-added" does not mean there is no sodium in a product. Check the nutrition information panel for the actual amount.

Next, check the package for the list of ingredients, keeping in mind that ingredients are listed in order of quantity. Avoid products where forms of fat or sugar are among the first ingredients listed. To save calories, look for alternative products that are lower in fat or sugar, such as low-sugar jams and jellies, juice-packed fruits, and seafood packed in water rather than in oil. Don't assume, however, that foods labeled "dietetic" are necessarily low in calories. Any product suitable for any one of a number of special diets, such as salt-free or diabetic, may be labeled dietetic.

Here are a few more tips for smart shopping: Look for lean cuts of meat, without a lot of fat marbled through the meat (unlike the fat around the edges, marbled fat can't be trimmed off). Skim milk or low-fat milk can provide the same amount of protein and calcium as whole milk, yet

ontain fewer calories and less saturated fat. Low-fat plain yogurt con-
ains only about half the calories of fruit yogurt. Look for cheeses that are
ower in fat, calories and sodium. Diet margarine contains half the
umber of calories of regular butter or margarine. Buy young frying
hickens and young turkeys; these usually have proportionately less fat
nd fewer calories per pound of meat than older birds. All of these are
ust examples of the general guideline—be aware of what you buy. You
an probably save hundreds of calories every week.

In addition, as simple as it may seem, make a shopping list before you
o to the store, and stick to it. Don't go shopping on an empty stomach.
)on't take friends or neighbors to the store with you—they can be a
istraction. And don't buy sale items or coupon items unless you really
eed them, and then only if they are nutritious, low in fat and low in
alories.

low to Use the Nutrition Figures for Each Recipe

very recipe in this book is accompanied by a listing of the nutrition
ontent for each serving. Included are figures for number of calories and
rams of protein, carbohydrate and fat, along with figures for milligrams
f cholesterol and sodium. The nutrition analysis for each recipe includes
ll the ingredients listed, except for those indicated as "optional." If an
ngredient is listed with one or more alternatives (for example, "1 cup
iced, cooked white-meat chicken or turkey"), the first item was used to
alculate the nutrition figures.

To relate the analysis for each recipe to recommended daily allow-
nces, refer to the following Nutrition Guidelines, which are based on
ecommendations for the general population by the National Academy
f Sciences, the U.S. Department of Agriculture and the American Heart
ssociation. The Average Daily Requirement for a Healthy Adult Female
s: 2,000 calories, 44 grams protein, 300 grams carbohydrate, 66 grams
at, 300 milligrams cholesterol, and 1,100 to 3,300 milligrams sodium.
he Average Daily Requirement for a Healthy Adult Male is: 2,700
alories, 56 grams protein, 405 grams carbohydrate, 90 grams fat, 300
nilligrams cholesterol, and 1,100 to 3,300 milligrams sodium. The basic
ecommendation is that protein provide 8 to 12 percent of daily calories,
arbohydrate provide 58 to 62 percent of daily calories, and fat provide
he remaining 30 percent of daily calorie intake.

Vhat This Book Does and Does Not Do

his book offers a collection of low-calorie, low-fat, low-cholesterol and
ow-sodium recipes that can be incorporated into your regular diet plan
o help start and maintain a stay-slender, stay-healthy life-style. This
ook is not intended, however, as a medically therapeutic cookbook that
akes the place of your doctor's recommendations for special diet modi-
ications. Also, make sure you review any exercise program with your
loctor.

GERMAN PUFF PANCAKE

1 cup all-purpose flour
½ teaspoon baking powder
½ teaspoon salt
1 cup skim milk
1¼ cups liquid egg substitute
2 teaspoons safflower or
    corn oil
3 cups fresh fruit (sliced
    peaches, nectarines,
    strawberries or
    blueberries)

Sift flour, baking powder and salt into mixing bowl. Stir in milk; gradually beat in egg substitute. Spray large skillet or metal-handled omelet pan with cooking spray. Wipe with safflower oil. Heat over moderate heat. Pour in batter all at once. Cook 1 minute. Transfer skillet to a preheated 425°F oven. Bake uncovered 20 minutes, or until pancake is golden and puffy. Top with fruit and slice into 6 wedges to serve.

Makes 6 servings

	Per Serving
Calories	170
Carbohydrate (g)	29
Protein (g)	10
Total Fat (g)	2
Cholesterol (mg)	1
Sodium (mg)	349

BREAKFAST & LUNCH

MANICOTTI-STYLE OMELET

1 cup liquid egg substitute
1 cup low-fat cottage cheese
1 tablespoon grated Romano cheese
1/2 teaspoon pizza seasoning or oregano
Pepper to taste (optional)
Chopped fresh parsley
1 can (8 ounces) no-salt-added tomato sauce

Spray medium nonstick skillet with cooking spray. Heat over moderate heat. Add egg substitute. Spread cottage cheese over surface of eggs and sprinkle with Romano, pizza seasoning and pepper. When egg mixture is set, fold omelet in half and turn. Cook over low heat until cheese is just heated through. Sprinkle with parsley. Remove to platter; cover and keep warm. Heat tomato sauce in the skillet over high heat; pour over omelet. Cut into thirds to serve.

Makes 3 servings

	Per Serving
Calories	141
Carbohydrate (g)	12
Protein (g)	20
Total Fat (g)	2
Cholesterol (mg)	5
Sodium (mg)	516

FRENCH SAUSAGE PATTIES

1 1/2 pounds lean boneless pork, trimmed of fat, ground
1/4 cup shaved ice
1/4 teaspoon pepper
1/4 teaspoon ground allspice
1/4 teaspoon paprika
1/8 teaspoon thyme

Combine all ingredients in a bowl and mix lightly. Shape into 12 patties. If not to be used immediately, wrap, label and store in freezer. This sausage is uncured. Frozen patties may be broiled or grilled without defrosting (be sure to cook until well done). Thawed or unfrozen patties can be fried in a large nonstick skillet sprayed with cooking spray. Cook over moderate heat, turning once, until brown on both sides and cooked through, with no trace of pinkness remaining.

WARNING: Do not taste raw or undercooked pork sausage for seasoning. If you would like to taste-test before completing the seasoning, fry a small sample.

Makes 12 patties

	Per Patty
Calories	102
Carbohydrate (g)	0
Protein (g)	11
Total Fat (g)	6
Cholesterol (mg)	38
Sodium (mg)	29

*Manicotti-Style Omelet (top),
French Sausage Patties (bottom)*

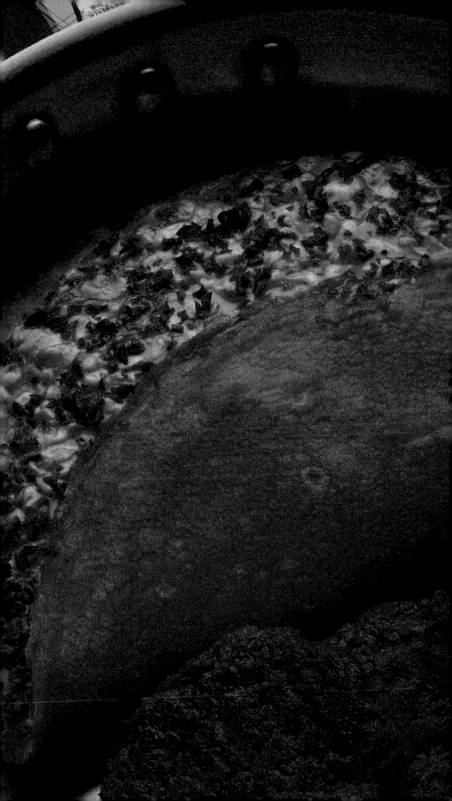

WHOLE-WHEAT PANCAKES

1¼ cups whole-wheat flour
2½ teaspoons baking powder
½ teaspoon salt
¼ cup liquid egg substitute
1¼ cups skim milk

Combine flour, baking powder and salt in mixing bowl. Mix together egg substitute and milk in separate bowl; stir into flour mixture until just moistened. (Batter will be lumpy.) Spray large nonstick skillet with cooking spray. Heat over moderate heat. Spoon the batter into hot skillet to make 4-inch pancakes. Cook over low heat until bubbles form on surface. Turn; cook other side until bottom is golden brown.

Makes 8 servings

	Per Serving
Calories	82
Carbohydrate (g)	16
Protein (g)	5
Total Fat (g)	0
Cholesterol (mg)	1
Sodium (mg)	307

HIGH-FIBER FRENCH TOAST

½ cup liquid egg substitute
¾ cup skim milk
1 teaspoon vanilla
½ teaspoon salt (optional)
8 slices high-fiber bread

Beat together egg substitute, milk, vanilla and salt in a bowl. Pour into shallow rectangular pan. Arrange bread in pan in single layer. Turn bread frequently with spatula until all slices are completely saturated with egg mixture. Spray large nonstick skillet with cooking spray. Heat over moderate heat. Brown bread slices in skillet over low heat on both sides.

Makes 8 slices

	Per Slice
Calories	72
Carbohydrate (g)	12
Protein (g)	5
Total Fat (g)	1
Cholesterol (mg)	0
Sodium (mg)	203

HIGH-FIBER BREAD QUICHE

4 slices high-fiber bread, preferably stale
1 cup low-fat cottage cheese
2 onions, minced
1 can (13 ounces) evaporated skim milk
¾ cup liquid egg substitute
1 tablespoon minced fresh parsley
Salt and pepper to taste (optional)
2 tablespoons bacon bits (optional)

Line 10-inch pie pan with bread. Spread with cottage cheese and onions. Combine remaining ingredients, except bacon bits, in blender. Cover; blend until smooth. Pour over onion layer. Sprinkle with bacon bits. Bake in a preheated 425°F oven 35 to 40 minutes, or until center is set and top is golden brown.

Makes 8 servings

	Per Serving
Calories	110
Carbohydrate (g)	14
Protein (g)	12
Total Fat (g)	1
Cholesterol (mg)	3
Sodium (mg)	305

MOCK CROQUE-MONSIEUR

1 slice high-fiber bread,
   toasted
2 ounces (2 slices) white-meat
   roast chicken or turkey
2 teaspoons reduced-calorie
   mayonnaise
½ ounce (1 thin slice) Swiss
   cheese

Spray flat broiler tray or
nonstick pie pan with cooking
spray. Place toast on tray; top with
chicken. Spread with mayonnaise
and top with cheese. Broil just
until cheese is melted. Slice
diagonally and serve immediately.

Makes 1 serving

Per Serving	
Calories	220
Carbohydrate (g)	11
Protein (g)	24
Total Fat (g)	9
Cholesterol (mg)	55
Sodium (mg)	309

BLENDER CHEESE PANCAKES

½ cup liquid egg substitute
1 cup low-fat cottage cheese
⅔ cup skim milk
½ teaspoon vanilla extract
1 cup sifted all-purpose flour
½ teaspoon baking soda
   Salt to taste (optional)

Combine egg substitute, cottage
cheese, milk and vanilla in
blender container. Cover; blend
until smooth. Add flour, baking
soda and salt. Blend on low speed
just until mixed. Spray large
nonstick skillet with cooking spray.
Heat over moderate heat. Spoon
the batter into hot skillet to make
4-inch pancakes. Cook over low
heat until bubbles form on
surface. Turn; cook other side until
bottom is golden brown.

Makes 8 servings

Per Serving	
Calories	91
Carbohydrate (g)	14
Protein (g)	7
Total Fat (g)	0
Cholesterol (mg)	2
Sodium (mg)	209

EGGLESS SALAD

1 cup liquid egg substitute
5 tablespoons reduced-calorie
   mayonnaise
2 tablespoons minced celery
2 tablespoons minced green
   bell pepper (optional)
1 tablespoon minced onion
½ teaspoon prepared mustard
   (optional)
   Salt and pepper to taste
   (optional)
   Dash red pepper sauce, or
   pinch red pepper
   (optional)

Cook egg substitute covered in
medium nonstick skillet over very
low heat 10 to 15 minutes, or
until the egg substitute thickens
and is set. Remove from heat and
cool slightly. Dice or shred the
cooked egg substitute. Combine
with remaining ingredients in a
bowl. Refrigerate.

Makes 4 servings

Per Serving	
Calories	92
Carbohydrate (g)	5
Protein (g)	7
Total Fat (g)	5
Cholesterol (mg)	6
Sodium (mg)	274

ASPARAGUS TIPS IN BLANKETS

32 fresh asparagus spears, or 2
   packages (10 ounces
   each) frozen asparagus
   spears, partly thawed
8 slices high-fiber white bread,
   trimmed of crusts
1 tablespoon reduced-calorie
   mayonnaise
2 tablespoons grated Romano
   cheese
2 teaspoons oregano
2 tablespoons safflower or corn
   oil
   Salt and pepper to taste
   (optional)
   Paprika

Choose uniform asparagus; cut
tips into 3-inch lengths (reserve
the rest to slice and add to soup
or stew). Steam asparagus in small
amount of water just until crisp-
tender. Cool.

Meanwhile, flatten bread with a
rolling pin. Cut each slice into 4
equal squares. Lightly dab each
square with mayonnaise; sprinkle
lightly with cheese and oregano.
Arrange an asparagus tip
diagonally on each bread square
and roll up. Arrange seam-side
down on nonstick baking sheet
sprayed with cooking spray. Brush
tops very lightly with oil. Sprinkle
with salt and pepper, if desired,
and paprika. Bake in a preheated
425°F oven until tops are crisp
and toasted. Serve warm.

Makes 32 appetizers

Per Serving	
Calories	26
Carbohydrate (g)	3
Protein (g)	1
Total Fat (g)	1
Cholesterol (mg)	0
Sodium (mg)	43

APPETIZERS

TUNA-STUFFED MUSHROOMS OR CELERY

(Photo on page 13)

2 cans (7 ounces each) water-packed white-meat tuna, drained
4 small stalks celery, cut into chunks
1 small onion, quartered, or 1 tablespoon onion flakes
3 tablespoons reduced-calorie mayonnaise
2 tablespoons fresh lemon juice
3 or 4 sprigs fresh parsley
Salt and pepper to taste (optional)
20 mushroom caps or 2-inch lengths of celery
Paprika (optional)
Minced fresh parsley (optional)

Combine tuna, 4 small stalks celery, onion, mayonnaise, lemon juice, parsley sprigs, salt and pepper in blender or food processor fitted with steel blade. Process until smooth. Spoon into mushroom caps or lengths of celery. Sprinkle with paprika and minced parsley, if desired.

Makes 20 appetizers

	Per Serving
Calories	29
Carbohydrate (g)	1
Protein (g)	5
Total Fat (g)	1
Cholesterol (mg)	11
Sodium (mg)	92

COTTAGE GUACAMOLE DIP

1 ripe avocado, halved, pitted
8 ounces low-fat cottage cheese
¼ cup chopped fresh parsley
1 small onion, quartered
1 tablespoon fresh lime juice
⅛ to ¼ teaspoon garlic powder

Scoop out avocado pulp; discard skin. Combine pulp with remaining ingredients in blender or food processor fitted with steel blade. Process until smooth. Cover and refrigerate until serving time. (Use as dip for fresh vegetables, cut into bite-size pieces.)

Makes about 2 cups

	Per Tablespoon
Calories	16
Carbohydrate (g)	1
Protein (g)	1
Total Fat (g)	1
Cholesterol (mg)	0
Sodium (mg)	30

LEAN "LIPTAUER" CHEESE SPREAD

1 cup low-fat cottage cheese
8 ounces Neufchâtel or low-fat cream cheese
1 tablespoon caraway seeds
1 tablespoon minced onion or chives
1 tablespoon minced fresh parsley
1 tablespoon capers (optional)
1 tablespoon paprika
1 teaspoon dry mustard
1 teaspoon Worcestershire sauce (optional)

Combine all ingredients in blender or food processor fitted with steel blade. Process until smooth. Spoon into large crock or shape into mound. Cover and refrigerate.

Makes 32 servings

	Per Serving
Calories	9
Carbohydrate (g)	0
Protein (g)	1
Total Fat (g)	0
Cholesterol (mg)	1
Sodium (mg)	32

TURKEY VERONICA

1 pound unsliced cooked turkey breast
32 seedless green grapes
1 cup reduced-calorie Roquefort or creamy Caesar dressing

Cut turkey into 1-inch cubes. Arrange 1 cube of turkey and 1 green grape on frilled party picks. Arrange around a bowl of salad dressing, for dipping.

Makes 32 appetizers

	Per Serving
Calories	36
Carbohydrate (g)	2
Protein (g)	5
Total Fat (g)	1
Cholesterol (mg)	10
Sodium (mg)	74

HAM AND MELON ON PARTY PICKS

1 ripe cantaloupe, halved, seeded
½ pound lean ready-to-eat low-sodium ham steak or unsliced Canadian bacon

Scoop melon with a melon baller, or quarter melon and slice into 1-inch cubes. Slice ham into 1-inch cubes. Arrange cube of melon and cube of ham on frilled party picks.

Makes 16 appetizers

	Per Serving
Calories	32
Carbohydrate (g)	3
Protein (g)	3
Total Fat (g)	1
Cholesterol (mg)	8
Sodium (mg)	117

SUNSHINE CHEESE BALL

1 can (8 ounces) juice-packed crushed pineapple, well drained
2 packages (8 ounces each) Neufchâtel or low-fat cream cheese, softened
6 tablespoons diced red or green bell pepper or 3 tablespoons of each
3 tablespoons minced purple onion
Salt and pepper to taste (optional)
½ cup plus 1 tablespoon unsalted sunflower seeds

Beat pineapple into cheese in a bowl until well blended. Fold in bell pepper and onion. Sprinkle with salt and pepper, if desired. Shape into a ball and roll in sunflower seeds. Cover and refrigerate until serving time.

Makes 32 servings

	Per Serving
Calories	56
Carbohydrate (g)	2
Protein (g)	2
Total Fat (g)	5
Cholesterol (mg)	11
Sodium (mg)	57

AMBROSIA FRUIT COCKTAIL

1 ripe banana, peeled, sliced
2 oranges, peeled, seeded, cut into chunks
1 can (8 ounces) juice-packed pineapple chunks, undrained
1 tablespoon undiluted frozen unsweetened pineapple juice concentrate, thawed
4 teaspoons flaked coconut

Combine fruits and juice concentrate in a bowl. Spoon into 4 stemmed glasses. Sprinkle with coconut.

Makes 4 servings

	Per Serving
Calories	80
Carbohydrate (g)	19
Protein (g)	1
Total Fat (g)	1
Cholesterol (mg)	0
Sodium (mg)	4

*Sunshine Cheese Ball (top),
Ambrosia Fruit Cocktail (bottom)*

MUSHROOM VINAIGRETTE SALAD

2 tablespoons safflower or
  corn oil
2 tablespoons white or cider
  vinegar
2 tablespoons water
1 tablespoon fresh lemon juice
1 tablespoon chopped fresh
  parsley
¼ teaspoon paprika
  Salt and pepper to taste
  (optional)
½ pound sliced fresh
  mushrooms
1 tablespoon capers (optional)
6 cups torn lettuce
1 tomato, cut in wedges
1 cup raw cauliflowerets

Beat together oil, vinegar, water,
lemon juice, parsley, paprika, salt
and pepper in small bowl. Add
mushrooms and capers; stir well.
Refrigerate several hours or
overnight. Place lettuce in bowl.
Arrange tomato wedges and
cauliflowerets in rings on top.
Remove mushrooms from
marinade and mound in center.
When ready to serve, pour
marinade over salad and toss
lightly to mix well.

Makes 6 servings

	Per Serving
Calories	71
Carbohydrate (g)	6
Protein (g)	2
Total Fat (g)	5
Cholesterol (mg)	0
Sodium (mg)	13

SOUPS & SALADS

LAMB-BARLEY SOUP

Meaty bone from roast leg
  of lamb
2 quarts water
¼ cup chopped fresh parsley
  Salt and pepper to taste
  (optional)
2 cups sliced carrots
2 cups sliced onions
2 cups sliced celery
1 can (16 ounces) no-salt-
  added tomatoes, well
  broken up, undrained
6 tablespoons medium pearl
  barley

Combine lamb bone, water,
parsley, salt and pepper in kettle.
Simmer covered 1 hour. Strain
broth; cool to room temperature.
Refrigerate until fat hardens;
remove and discard fat. Separate
meat from bones; discard bones.
Wrap and refrigerate meat. Stir
vegetables and barley into broth.
Simmer, covered, 1½ hours, or
until barley is tender. Stir in
reserved meat and heat through.
Makes 10 servings

Per Serving	
Calories	130
Carbohydrate (g)	13
Protein (g)	12
Total Fat (g)	2
Cholesterol (mg)	28
Sodium (mg)	99

SPANISH CHICKEN SOUP

2½ pounds frying chicken, cut
  up
6 cups water
1 can (16 ounces) no-salt-
  added tomatoes, cut up,
  undrained
1 onion, sliced
3 small carrots, sliced
3 stalks celery, sliced
1 bay leaf
  Salt and pepper to taste
  (optional)
1 small zucchini, diced
1 red or green bell pepper,
  sliced

Combine chicken and water in
kettle. Simmer covered 1 hour or
until chicken is tender. Remove
chicken from broth; reserve. Cool
broth to room temperature.
Refrigerate broth until fat hardens;
remove and discard fat. When
chicken is cool, remove and
discard skin and bones. Cube
chicken meat. Stir tomatoes,
onion, carrots, celery, bay leaf,
salt and pepper into broth.
Simmer covered about 30
minutes, or until carrots are
tender. Stir chicken, zucchini and
red pepper into broth. Simmer,
covered, 6 to 8 minutes, or until
zucchini is tender. Remove bay
leaf.
Makes 8 meal-size servings

Per Serving	
Calories	129
Carbohydrate (g)	7
Protein (g)	16
Total Fat (g)	4
Cholesterol (mg)	45
Sodium (mg)	73

TRIM TURKEY SOUP

1 small meaty turkey carcass
6 cups water
1 bay leaf
1/8 teaspoon ground nutmeg
  Salt and pepper to taste
  (optional)
3 small carrots, diced or sliced
4 stalks celery, diced or sliced
2 onions, sliced

Combine turkey carcass, water, bay leaf, nutmeg, salt and pepper in kettle. Heat to boiling; reduce heat. Simmer covered about 2 hours. Strain broth; cool to room temperature. Refrigerate broth until fat hardens; remove and discard fat. Separate meat from bones; reserve meat. Discard bones and skin. Stir meat and vegetables into broth. Simmer, covered, 25 to 30 minutes, or until vegetables are tender.

Makes 6 servings

	Per Serving
Calories	126
Carbohydrate (g)	6
Protein (g)	17
Total Fat (g)	2
Cholesterol (mg)	36
Sodium (mg)	122

"CREAM" OF MUSHROOM SOUP

1 pound fresh mushrooms
4 cups fat-skimmed chicken
  broth, low-sodium canned
  or homemade
1 can (13 ounces) evaporated
  skim milk
1/2 cup cold water
3 tablespoons instant-blend
  flour
  Salt and pepper to taste
  (optional)
  Chopped fresh parsley
  (optional)

Remove and chop mushroom stems. Reserve caps. Combine chopped stems with broth in saucepan. Simmer, covered, over very low heat 30 minutes. Strain broth; discard stems. Return broth to saucepan; heat to boiling. Reduce heat; stir in the milk and heat until simmering. In small cup, mix water and flour into smooth paste; stir into simmering soup. Continue to cook and stir over low heat until soup is slightly thickened. Thinly slice reserved mushroom caps; stir into soup. Simmer 6 to 8 minutes. Sprinkle with salt and pepper and garnish with parsley, if desired.

Makes 6 servings

	Per Serving
Calories	102
Carbohydrate (g)	14
Protein (g)	9
Total Fat (g)	0
Cholesterol (mg)	3
Sodium (mg)	119

MINESTRONE WITH MEATBALLS

½ pound lean beef round,
   trimmed of fat, ground
Garlic powder to taste
Pepper to taste
2 onions, thinly sliced
1 can (19 ounces) no-salt-
   added minestrone soup
½ teaspoon oregano or mixed
   Italian seasoning
2 tablespoons grated Romano
   cheese (optional)

Sprinkle meat with garlic powder and pepper in a bowl; mix lightly. Shape into 1-inch meatballs. Brown on all sides under broiler. Combine meatballs, onions, soup and oregano in saucepan. Simmer covered until onions are tender. Pour into 2 soup bowls and sprinkle with cheese, if desired.

Makes 2 meal-size servings

	Per Serving
Calories	391
Carbohydrate (g)	39
Protein (g)	30
Total Fat (g)	12
Cholesterol (mg)	79
Sodium (mg)	182

"CREAM" OF POTATO SOUP

3 potatoes, pared, sliced
1 onion, minced
2 cups fat-skimmed chicken
   broth, low-sodium canned
   or homemade
1½ cups water
1 can (13 ounces) evaporated
   skim milk
Salt and white pepper to
   taste (optional)
3 tablespoons minced chives
   (optional)

Combine potatoes, onion, broth and water in saucepan. Simmer covered 35 minutes. Pour into blender. Cover; blend until smooth. Return to saucepan and heat to boiling. Stir in milk. Reduce heat and simmer covered 4 to 5 minutes. Sprinkle with salt and pepper and garnish with chives, if desired.

Makes 8 servings

	Per Serving
Calories	83
Carbohydrate (g)	14
Protein (g)	5
Total Fat (g)	0
Cholesterol (mg)	2
Sodium (mg)	76

Minestrone with Meatballs

CHICKEN OR TURKEY SALAD HAWAIIAN-STYLE

2 cups diced cooked white-
    meat chicken or turkey
1 cup chopped celery
1 cup juice-packed pineapple
    chunks, drained
¼ cup pineapple juice (from
    can)
¼ cup reduced-calorie
    mayonnaise
    Salt and pepper to taste
    (optional)
    Lettuce (optional)

Combine all ingredients in a
bowl, except lettuce, and toss
lightly. Refrigerate until cold.
Serve on lettuce, if desired.

Makes 4 servings

Per Serving	
Calories	200
Carbohydrate (g)	12
Protein (g)	23
Total Fat (g)	7
Cholesterol (mg)	65
Sodium (mg)	192

BEEF STROGANOFF SALAD

1 pound leftover lean broiled
    beef round steak or roast
    beef
¼ cup dry white wine
3 tablespoons white vinegar
2 tablespoons no-salt-added
    catsup
1 teaspoon dry mustard
4 potatoes, pared, cooked,
    diced (cooked without
    salt)
2 cups sliced fresh
    mushrooms

¾ cup low-fat plain yogurt
1 red onion, halved, thinly
    sliced

Trim all fat from meat. Slice
meat thinly against grain into bite-
size pieces. Combine meat with
wine, vinegar, catsup and mustard
in a bowl. Marinate at least 1 hour
in refrigerator. Stir in remaining
ingredients and refrigerate.

Makes 6 servings

Per Serving	
Calories	254
Carbohydrate (g)	23
Protein (g)	27
Total Fat (g)	5
Cholesterol (mg)	71
Sodium (mg)	85

MARINATED CUCUMBERS

½ cup low-fat plain yogurt
2 tablespoons fresh lemon
    juice
1 teaspoon sugar (optional)
    Salt and pepper to taste
    (optional)
2 cucumbers, pared, thinly
    sliced

Combine yogurt, lemon juice,
sugar, salt and pepper in a bowl.
Toss with cucumbers; refrigerate.

Makes 4 servings

Per Serving	
Calories	39
Carbohydrate (g)	7
Protein (g)	2
Total Fat (g)	1
Cholesterol (mg)	2
Sodium (mg)	24

CRAB AND MUSHROOM SALAD

½ head iceberg lettuce, torn into bite-size pieces
1 cup (5 to 6 ounces) fresh (cooked, drained), or frozen (thawed, drained) Alaskan king crab
¼ pound fresh mushrooms, quartered (about 1½ cups)
1 large tomato, cut into wedges
1 tablespoon fresh lemon juice
2 teaspoons safflower or corn oil
Salt and pepper to taste (optional)

Arrange lettuce in 2 large bowls. Combine remaining ingredients in third bowl; divide between lettuce-lined bowls. Toss lightly.

Makes 2 servings

Per Serving	
Calories	184
Carbohydrate (g)	15
Protein (g)	18
Total Fat (g)	7
Cholesterol (mg)	78
Sodium (mg)	194

MUSHROOM AND TURKEY CLUB SALAD

3 or 4 lettuce leaves
½ cup diced cooked turkey
4 fresh mushrooms, sliced
½ cup cooked fresh green beans (cooked without salt)
4 cherry tomatoes, cut into halves
5 cucumber slices

1 tablespoon cocktail vegetable juice
1 tablespoon fresh lemon juice
1 teaspoon safflower or corn oil
Salt to taste (optional)
Dash red pepper sauce

Line bowl with lettuce leaves. Place turkey in center of bowl. Surround with separate clusters of each of the vegetables. Combine vegetable juice, lemon juice, oil, salt, if desired, and red pepper sauce in small bowl; pour over salad.

Makes 1 serving

Per Serving	
Calories	212
Carbohydrate (g)	12
Protein (g)	24
Total Fat (g)	8
Cholesterol (mg)	54
Sodium (mg)	118

COTTAGE-STYLE TUNA SALAD

½ cup low-fat cottage cheese
1 can (7 ounces) low-sodium water-packed tuna, drained
½ small green bell pepper, diced
¼ cup diced celery
1 tablespoon minced chives
1 teaspoon fresh lemon juice
Pepper to taste (optional)

Combine ingredients in bowl; toss lightly to mix. (Serve on lettuce or in sandwiches.)

Makes 6 servings

Per Serving	
Calories	52
Carbohydrate (g)	1
Protein (g)	10
Total Fat (g)	1
Cholesterol (mg)	11
Sodium (mg)	92

CHEF'S SALAD MOLD

2 envelopes unflavored gelatin
2½ cups cold water
½ cup sugar
½ teaspoon salt or to taste
  (optional)
½ cup cider vinegar
2 tablespoons fresh lemon
  juice
1 cup shredded no-salt-added
  Swiss cheese
1 cup finely diced low-sodium
  cooked ham
¾ cup diced green bell pepper
¾ cup thinly sliced celery
  Lettuce (optional)

Sprinkle gelatin over 1 cup of the cold water in saucepan. Let stand 1 minute to soften. Add sugar. Place over low heat; cook, stirring constantly, until gelatin dissolves. Remove from heat. Stir in salt, if desired. Add remaining 1½ cups cold water. Stir in vinegar and lemon juice. Refrigerate until mixture is slightly thickened. Fold in remaining ingredients, except lettuce. Turn into 6-cup mold or individual molds. Refrigerate until firm. Unmold on lettuce, if desired.

Makes 6 servings

Per Serving	
Calories	183
Carbohydrate (g)	20
Protein (g)	13
Total Fat (g)	7
Cholesterol (mg)	13
Sodium (mg)	213

POLYNESIAN SHRIMP-STUFFED PAPAYA

1 ripe fresh papaya
½ pound fresh shrimp, cooked,
  shelled, deveined, or ½
  pound cooked diced
  chicken or turkey breast
¼ cup reduced-calorie
  mayonnaise
2 tablespoons finely chopped
  green onion
2 tablespoons low-fat plain
  yogurt
1 tablespoon fresh lemon juice

Slice papaya lengthwise in half. Scoop out and discard seeds. Cover and refrigerate. Combine remaining ingredients in a bowl and mix well. Refrigerate until cold. At serving time, mound shrimp mixture in papaya halves. (Or place shrimp in papaya halves. Mix remaining ingredients; top shrimp with mixture.)

Makes 2 servings

Per Serving	
Calories	244
Carbohydrate (g)	22
Protein (g)	19
Total Fat (g)	9
Cholesterol (mg)	150
Sodium (mg)	372

Chef's Salad Mold (top),
Polynesian Shrimp-Stuffed Papaya (bottom)

CURRIED FRUIT DRESSING

1 cup low-fat plain yogurt
3 tablespoons golden raisins
2 tablespoons thawed,
  undiluted, unsweetened
  frozen pineapple juice
  concentrate
½ teaspoon grated lemon rind
½ teaspoon curry powder
½ teaspoon ground cinnamon

Combine all ingredients in a
bowl; mix well. Store covered in
refrigerator.

Makes 1¼ cups

Per Tablespoon	
Calories	15
Carbohydrate (g)	3
Protein (g)	1
Total Fat (g)	0
Cholesterol (mg)	1
Sodium (mg)	8

CREAMY SALAD DRESSING

¼ cup reduced-calorie
  mayonnaise
¼ cup white or cider vinegar
¼ cup cold water

Combine all ingredients in jar.
Cover and shake well. Store in
refrigerator. (For an Italian version
of this recipe, add ½ teaspoon
oregano and pinch onion powder
or garlic powder.)

Makes ¾ cup

Per Tablespoon	
Calories	14
Carbohydrate (g)	1
Protein (g)	0
Total Fat (g)	1
Cholesterol (mg)	2
Sodium (mg)	38

SEAFOOD DRESSING

1 cup low-fat plain yogurt
1 cup reduced-calorie
  mayonnaise
½ cup spicy chili sauce
2 tablespoons fresh lemon
  juice
1 tablespoon minced onion
1 tablespoon prepared
  horseradish
  Pinch tarragon
  Salt and pepper to taste
  (optional)

Combine all ingredients in bowl;
mix well. Store in refrigerator.

Makes 2¾ cups

Per Tablespoon	
Calories	22
Carbohydrate (g)	2
Protein (g)	0
Total Fat (g)	2
Cholesterol (mg)	2
Sodium (mg)	86

PARSLEY DRESSING

1 cup low-fat plain yogurt
3 tablespoons minced fresh
  parsley
1 teaspoon dillweed
⅛ teaspoon garlic powder
  (optional)

Combine all ingredients in a
bowl; mix well. Store in
refrigerator.

Makes 1 cup

Per Tablespoon	
Calories	9
Carbohydrate (g)	1
Protein (g)	1
Total Fat (g)	0
Cholesterol (mg)	1
Sodium (mg)	10

MOCK MAYONNAISE

1 cup low-fat cottage cheese
¼ cup liquid egg substitute
1 tablespoon white vinegar or
  fresh lemon juice
2 teaspoons sugar
½ teaspoon salt (optional)
½ teaspoon dry mustard
½ teaspoon paprika
  Pinch pepper

Combine all ingredients in blender. Cover and blend on medium speed until smooth, scraping down container with rubber spatula as needed. Store in covered container in refrigerator.

Makes 1 cup

	Per Tablespoon
Calories	15
Carbohydrate (g)	1
Protein (g)	2
Total Fat (g)	0
Cholesterol (mg)	1
Sodium (mg)	65

YOGURT DRESSING

1 cup low-fat plain yogurt
3 tablespoons fresh lemon
  juice
⅛ teaspoon dry mustard
  Salt and pepper to taste
  (optional)
  Pinch garlic powder

Combine all ingredients in jar. Cover and shake well. Store in refrigerator.

Makes 1¼ cups

	Per Tablespoon
Calories	8
Carbohydrate (g)	1
Protein (g)	1
Total Fat (g)	1
Cholesterol (mg)	1
Sodium (mg)	8

ORANGE DRESSING

½ cup fresh orange juice
¼ cup fresh lemon juice
½ teaspoon paprika
⅛ teaspoon garlic powder
  (optional)
⅛ teaspoon pepper

Combine all ingredients in jar. Cover and shake well. Store in refrigerator.

Makes ¾ cup

	Per Tablespoon
Calories	7
Carbohydrate (g)	2
Protein (g)	0
Total Fat (g)	0
Cholesterol (mg)	0
Sodium (mg)	0

CREAMY CAESAR SALAD DRESSING

⅓ cup reduced-calorie
  mayonnaise
¼ cup fresh lemon juice
¼ cup water
2 tablespoons grated
  Parmesan cheese
  (optional)
1 clove garlic, finely chopped
  Dash Worcestershire sauce
  Salt and pepper to taste
  (optional)

Combine all ingredients in jar; cover and shake well. Or combine ingredients in bowl; beat until well blended. Store in refrigerator.

Makes ¾ cup

	Per Tablespoon
Calories	19
Carbohydrate (g)	1
Protein (g)	0
Total Fat (g)	2
Cholesterol (mg)	2
Sodium (mg)	51

CORNISH HENS WITH CHERRIES

4 Rock Cornish hens (about 4 pounds total), cut into halves lengthwise
1 can (16 ounces) juice-packed dark cherries, drained, juice reserved
¼ teaspoon poultry seasoning
Salt and pepper to taste (optional)
½ cup bottled unsweetened red grape juice
Water
2 teaspoons cornstarch or arrowroot

Broil hen halves, skin-side up, 10 to 15 minutes, or until skin is crisp. Pour off fat. Blot hen halves with paper towels. Place skin-side up in shallow baking dish. Pour ½ cup of the reserved juice from the cherries over hen halves. Sprinkle with poultry seasoning and salt and pepper, if desired. Bake in preheated 350°F oven, basting frequently, about 1 hour, or until hen halves are tender. Meanwhile, pour remaining cherry juice into 2-cup measure; add grape juice and enough water to measure 1¾ cups liquid. Stir liquid and cornstarch in saucepan until smooth. Cook and stir over low heat until mixture thickens and clears. Stir in cherries and heat through. Pour sauce over hens and serve.

Makes 8 servings

Per Serving	
Calories	281
Carbohydrate (g)	11
Protein (g)	28
Total Fat (g)	14
Cholesterol (mg)	88
Sodium (mg)	84

MAIN DISHES

COQ AU VIN ROUGE

1 frying chicken (about 2
   pounds), cup up, trimmed
   of fat
1 cup fresh or frozen small
   onions
¾ cup dry red wine
¼ cup no-salt-added tomato
   juice
1 small bay leaf
⅛ teaspoon thyme
⅛ teaspoon sage
   Salt and pepper to taste
   (optional)

Broil chicken pieces, skin-side
up, 10 to 15 minutes, or until skin
is crisp. Pour off fat. Blot chicken
with paper towels. Combine with
remaining ingredients in heavy
Dutch oven. Cover and simmer
over moderate heat or bake in a
preheated 350°F oven 45 to 50
minutes, or until chicken is tender.
Uncover and continue to cook
until liquid is reduced to a thick
sauce. Remove bay leaf.

Makes 4 servings

Per Serving	
Calories	266
Carbohydrate (g)	7
Protein (g)	28
Total Fat (g)	14
Cholesterol (mg)	88
Sodium (mg)	90

TURKEY STEAKS WITH MUSHROOMS

1 pound turkey breast steaks
1 tablespoon diet margarine
2 cups sliced fresh
   mushrooms
½ cup sherry
   Salt and pepper to taste
   (optional)

Sauté steaks in margarine in
nonstick skillet until done.
Remove to serving platter. Sauté
mushrooms in skillet; stir in sherry
and salt and pepper, if desired.
Cook 2 to 3 minutes. Top steaks
with mushroom mixture.

Makes 4 servings

Per Serving	
Calories	161
Carbohydrate (g)	4
Protein (g)	27
Total Fat (g)	3
Cholesterol (mg)	70
Sodium (mg)	113

"SOUTHERN FRIED" CHICKEN

2 frying chickens (about 2
   pounds each), cut up,
   trimmed of fat
   Water
½ cup plain bread crumbs
½ teaspoon paprika
¼ teaspoon salt
¼ teaspoon marjoram
¼ teaspoon thyme
   Pinch pepper

Brush chicken pieces with water
to moisten. Combine remaining
ingredients in heavy paper bag.
Place chicken pieces, a few at a
time, in paper bag; shake to coat
chicken. Arrange skin-side up in
nonstick pan or baking sheet.
Bake in preheated 375°F oven
about 50 minutes, or until chicken
is tender.

Makes 8 servings

Per Serving	
Calories	264
Carbohydrate (g)	5
Protein (g)	28
Total Fat (g)	14
Cholesterol (mg)	88
Sodium (mg)	196

CHICKEN CACCIATORE

3 whole chicken breasts
   (about 2 pounds), split,
   trimmed of fat
1 can (16 ounces) no-salt-
   added tomatoes,
   undrained, cut up
1 green bell pepper, sliced
½ cup dry white wine
1 to 2 teaspoons oregano
   Salt and pepper to taste
   (optional)
2 tablespoons grated Romano
   cheese

Broil chicken, skin-side up, 10 to 15 minutes, or until skin is crisp. Pour off fat. Blot chicken with paper towels. Mix together remaining ingredients, except cheese, in skillet. Add chicken. Cover and simmer over moderate heat 45 to 50 minutes, or until chicken is tender. Uncover; cook until pan juices are reduced to sauce consistency. Sprinkle with cheese before serving.

Makes 6 servings

Per Serving	
Calories	191
Carbohydrate (g)	5
Protein (g)	26
Total Fat (g)	7
Cholesterol (mg)	70
Sodium (mg)	89

CHICKEN NOODLE STROGANOFF

2 pounds chicken thighs,
   trimmed of fat
¾ cup no-salt-added tomato
   juice
1 onion, chopped
1 can (4 ounces) sliced
   mushrooms, undrained
¼ teaspoon dry mustard
½ cup skim milk
½ cup low-fat plain yogurt
2 tablespoons instant-blend
   flour
   Salt and pepper to taste
   (optional)
4 cups tender-cooked wide
   noodles

Broil chicken, skin-side up, 10 to 15 minutes, or until skin is crisp. Pour off fat. Blot chicken with paper towels. Combine tomato juice, onion, mushrooms and mustard in large saucepan; add chicken. Cover and simmer about 50 minutes, or until chicken is tender, adding water if needed. Skim off fat. Mix together milk, yogurt and flour in a bowl until smooth; stir into saucepan. Cook and stir until sauce simmers and thickens. Sprinkle with salt and pepper, if desired. Serve over hot noodles.

Makes 6 servings

Per Serving	
Calories	371
Carbohydrate (g)	31
Protein (g)	27
Total Fat (g)	14
Cholesterol (mg)	108
Sodium (mg)	171

CHICKEN CORDON BLEU

4 whole chicken breasts
(about 2 pounds), split,
skinned and boned
8 teaspoons chopped fresh
parsley
8 thin slices (4 ounces) part-
skim mozzarella cheese
4 thin slices (4 ounces) low-
sodium boiled ham, cut
into halves
1 tablespoon reduced-calorie
mayonnaise
1 tablespoon warm water
¼ cup seasoned bread crumbs

Pound chicken breasts until
they are thin. Lay out flat and
sprinkle with parsley. Top each
breast with a slice of cheese, then
a half-slice of ham. Roll up tightly.
Stir together mayonnaise and
water in shallow dish. Roll each
chicken breast in the mayonnaise
mixture, then in the bread
crumbs. Spray a baking sheet with
cooking spray. Arrange the
chicken rolls, seam-side down, in
single layer on baking sheet. Bake
in a preheated 425°F oven 15 to
20 minutes, or until browned,
cooked through and cheese is
melted.

Makes 8 servings

	Per Serving
Calories	200
Carbohydrate (g)`	3
Protein (g)	33
Total Fat (g)	5
Cholesterol (mg)	82
Sodium (mg)	368

WHITE WINE SAUCE

1 cup fat-skimmed chicken or
turkey broth, low-sodium
canned or homemade
3 tablespoons dry white wine
3 tablespoons instant-blend
flour
⅔ cup skim milk
Onion powder and white
pepper to taste (optional)
Pinch ground nutmeg
(optional)
1 tablespoon minced fresh
parsley

Combine broth and wine in
nonstick saucepan. Heat to boiling;
reduce heat. Mix together flour
and milk in small cup until
smooth; stir into simmering broth.
Cook and stir until mixture is thick
and bubbling. Sprinkle with onion
powder, pepper and nutmeg, if
desired. Thin with a little water, if
necessary. Sprinkle with parsley.

Makes about 2 cups

	Per ¼ Cup
Calories	22
Carbohydrate (g)	3
Protein (g)	1
Total Fat (g)	0
Cholesterol (mg)	0
Sodium (mg)	18

*Chicken Cordon Bleu
with White Wine Sauce*

HUNGARIAN TURKEY SKILLET

1¼ pounds turkey thigh, skinned, boned, cut into ¼-inch cubes
1 onion, cut into strips
2 green bell peppers, cut into strips
1 red bell pepper, cut into strips
2 tomatoes, peeled, seeded, diced
1 cup water
   Salt and pepper to taste (optional)
   Pinch cayenne pepper or to taste

Combine all ingredients in heavy skillet. Cover and simmer 35 minutes, or until meat is tender. Uncover and continue to simmer until sauce is thick.

Makes 4 servings

Per Serving	
Calories	157
Carbohydrate (g)	12
Protein (g)	18
Total Fat (g)	4
Cholesterol (mg)	60
Sodium (mg)	73

THOUSAND ISLAND CHICKEN THIGHS

2 pounds chicken thighs, trimmed of fat
⅓ cup reduced-calorie Thousand Island salad dressing
¼ cup unsweetened pineapple juice
¼ cup dry white wine

Place chicken in plastic bag or large bowl. Mix together remaining ingredients in another bowl; pour over chicken. Marinate 30 minutes at room temperature or several hours in refrigerator, turning frequently. Place chicken, skin-side up, in shallow baking dish; pour marinade over chicken. Bake in preheated 350°F oven, basting occasionally, 35 to 45 minutes, or until tender.

Makes 6 servings

Per Serving	
Calories	215
Carbohydrate (g)	4
Protein (g)	20
Total Fat (g)	13
Cholesterol (mg)	73
Sodium (mg)	67

CHICKEN TERIYAKI

3 whole chicken breasts (about 2 pounds), split, trimmed of fat
½ cup dry white wine
¼ cup water
3 tablespoons low-sodium soy sauce
¼ teaspoon ground ginger
⅛ teaspoon garlic powder

Place chicken in glass or ceramic bowl. Mix together remaining ingredients in a bowl; pour over chicken. Cover and marinate several hours or overnight in refrigerator. Drain and reserve marinade. Grill or broil chicken 10 inches from heat, turning once, about 30 minutes or until tender. Baste frequently with reserved marinade.

Makes 6 servings

Per Serving	
Calories	170
Carbohydrate (g)	1
Protein (g)	25
Total Fat (g)	6
Cholesterol (mg)	69
Sodium (mg)	362

CHICKEN-STUFFED ACORN SQUASH

2 small acorn squash (¾
    pound each), halved,
    seeded
½ cup fat-skimmed chicken
    broth, low-sodium canned
    or homemade
½ cup skim milk
2 tablespoons instant-blend
    flour
1 tablespoon instant minced
    onion
1 teaspoon parsley flakes
2 cups cooked white-meat
    chicken, diced
    Salt and pepper to taste
    (optional)
    Poultry seasoning to taste
    (optional)

Place squash halves, cut-sides down, on baking sheet. Bake in preheated 400°F oven about 30 minutes, or until tender. Meanwhile, combine broth, milk, flour, onion and parsley in saucepan. Cook and stir until sauce boils and thickens. Stir in chicken and heat through. Sprinkle with salt, pepper and poultry seasoning, if desired. Spoon into squash halves and serve.

Makes 4 servings

Per Serving	
Calories	199
Carbohydrate (g)	19
Protein (g)	25
Total Fat (g)	3
Cholesterol (mg)	61
Sodium (mg)	79

TURKEY-CHEESE ROLL

1¼ pounds turkey thigh, boned
    Garlic powder and pepper to
    taste (optional)
3 tablespoons minced onion
4 thin slices (2 ounces) sharp
    Cheddar cheese
3 tablespoons chopped fresh
    parsley
1 cup no-salt-added tomato
    juice
2 teaspoons Worcestershire
    sauce
    Dash red pepper sauce
    (optional)

Lay turkey meat flat, skin-side down. Sprinkle with garlic powder, pepper and onion. Arrange cheese slices over meat; sprinkle with parsley. Roll up tightly. Place roll in baking dish just large enough to hold it (so that it will not unroll). Combine tomato juice, Worcestershire and pepper sauce in a bowl; pour over turkey roll. Bake covered in preheated 350°F oven, basting occasionally, 2½ to 3 hours, or until tender. Uncover during the last hour of baking. Slice to serve.

Makes 4 servings

Per Serving	
Calories	173
Carbohydrate (g)	4
Protein (g)	20
Total Fat (g)	8
Cholesterol (mg)	75
Sodium (mg)	187

CHICKEN PORTUGUAISE

1 frying chicken (about 2 pounds), cut up, trimmed of fat
1 onion, thinly sliced
1 large or 2 small bell peppers, thinly sliced
¼ pound fresh mushrooms, thinly sliced
1 stalk celery, chopped
1 can (16 ounces) no-salt-added tomatoes, undrained, cut up
¼ cup rosé or white wine
4 cloves garlic, minced
Salt and pepper to taste (optional)

Broil chicken pieces, skin-side up, 10 to 15 minutes, or until skin is crisp. Pour off fat. Blot chicken with paper towels. Place onion, bell pepper, mushrooms and celery in shallow baking dish. Arrange chicken over vegetables. Mix together tomatoes, wine, garlic, salt and pepper in a bowl; pour over chicken. Bake in preheated 400°F oven, basting frequently, 50 to 60 minutes, or until chicken is tender and sauce is thick.

Makes 4 servings

	Per Serving
Calories	293
Carbohydrate (g)	12
Protein (g)	30
Total Fat (g)	14
Cholesterol (mg)	88
Sodium (mg)	109

ORIENTAL CHICKEN

2 frying chickens (about 1½ pounds each), cut up, trimmed of fat
1 can (16 ounces) juice-packed pineapple chunks, drained, juice reserved
3 tablespoons wine vinegar
2 tablespoons low-sodium soy sauce
1 teaspoon prepared mustard
1 red bell pepper, cut into strips
1 green bell pepper, cut into strips
2 teaspoons cornstarch or arrowroot
¼ cup water

Broil chicken pieces, skin-side up, 10 to 15 minutes, or until skin is crisp. Pour off fat. Blot chicken with paper towels. Place chicken, skin-side up, in shallow baking dish; surround with pineapple chunks. Mix reserved juice, vinegar, soy sauce and mustard in a bowl; pour over chicken. Bake in preheated 325°F oven, basting occasionally, 40 minutes. Add pepper strips. Stir cornstarch into water in a small cup until smooth; stir into liquid in baking dish. Bake 15 minutes, or until thick and bubbling.

Makes 8 servings

	Per Serving
Calories	226
Carbohydrate (g)	11
Protein (g)	21
Total Fat (g)	10
Cholesterol (mg)	66
Sodium (mg)	223

VEAL ROMANOFF

1 tablespoon diet margarine
1½ pounds veal for scaloppine,
    cut into 1-inch strips
½ cup sliced onion
⅓ cup dry white wine
⅓ cup tomato juice
1 teaspoon prepared mustard
2 tablespoons instant-blend
    flour
½ cup low-fat plain yogurt
    Salt and pepper to taste
    (optional)
3 tablespoons grated Romano
    cheese
2 tablespoons minced fresh
    parsley
    Cooked rice or noodles
    (optional)

Melt margarine in large nonstick skillet. Add veal strips and brown quickly over high heat, stirring constantly. Add onion, wine, tomato juice and mustard. Reduce heat and simmer covered 10 minutes, or until onion is tender. Mix together flour and yogurt in small cup until smooth; stir into simmering liquid. Cook and stir until sauce is thick. Season to taste with salt and pepper, if desired. Sprinkle with cheese and garnish with parsley. Serve from skillet (over rice or noodles, if desired).

Makes 6 servings

	Per Serving
Calories	235
Carbohydrate (g)	6
Protein (g)	25
Total Fat (g)	12
Cholesterol (mg)	84
Sodium (mg)	204

VEAL AND MUSHROOMS IN WINE

2 pounds lean veal shoulder,
    trimmed of fat, cut into
    1-inch cubes
1 tablespoon safflower or corn
    oil
1 onion, sliced
1 clove garlic, minced
    Salt and pepper to taste
    (optional)
¾ cup dry white wine
½ pound fresh mushrooms,
    sliced
2 tablespoons chopped fresh
    parsley

Brown meat in hot oil in large nonstick skillet. Add onion, garlic, salt, pepper and wine. Cover and simmer 45 minutes, or until meat is almost tender. Stir in mushrooms. Simmer, covered, 15 minutes. Sprinkle with parsley.

Makes 8 servings

	Per Serving
Calories	226
Carbohydrate (g)	3
Protein (g)	23
Total Fat (g)	13
Cholesterol (mg)	81
Sodium (mg)	80

PACIFIC VEAL ON SKEWERS

1 tablespoon all-purpose flour
½ teaspoon marjoram
  Salt and pepper to taste
  (optional)
1 cup unsweetened pineapple
  juice
2 tablespoons low-sodium soy
  sauce
¼ cup chopped onion
1 clove garlic, minced
2 pounds boneless veal rump,
  cut into 1¼-inch cubes
¾ cup juice-packed pineapple
  chunks, drained
2 bell peppers (1 red, 1 green),
  cut into squares
1 tablespoon safflower or corn
  oil

Combine flour, marjoram, salt and pepper in saucepan. Stir in pineapple juice, soy sauce, onion and garlic. Heat to boiling; reduce heat. Simmer 10 minutes, stirring occasionally. Cool. Pour marinade over cubed veal in large bowl. Refrigerate covered 4 to 6 hours, or overnight. Drain veal, reserving marinade. Thread veal cubes on four 12-inch skewers alternately with pineapple and bell pepper. Broil or grill, 5 to 6 inches from heat, brushing with oil and reserved marinade and turning frequently, 25 to 30 minutes, or until done as desired.

Makes 8 servings

Per Serving	
Calories	235
Carbohydrate (g)	11
Protein (g)	23
Total Fat (g)	11
Cholesterol (mg)	81
Sodium (mg)	206

BEEF-PORK-VEAL LOAF

1 pound lean beef round,
  trimmed of fat, ground
½ pound lean pork, trimmed of
  fat, ground
½ pound lean veal, ground
1 can (16 ounces) no-salt-
  added tomatoes, drained,
  chopped
1 green bell pepper, chopped
1 onion, chopped
2 tablespoons chopped fresh
  parsley
2 teaspoons oregano or mixed
  Italian seasoning
1 tablespoon fresh lemon juice
1 teaspoon fennel seeds
  Garlic powder and pepper to
  taste (optional)

Mix all ingredients thoroughly in a bowl. Shape into a loaf. Place on rack in baking pan. Bake in a preheated 350°F oven 1 hour, or until loaf is cooked through.

Makes 8 servings

Per Serving	
Calories	168
Carbohydrate (g)	5
Protein (g)	21
Total Fat (g)	7
Cholesterol (mg)	63
Sodium (mg)	139

Pacific Veal on Skewers

ITALIAN FLANK STEAK

1½ pounds lean flank steak
  1 cup sliced fresh mushrooms
  1 small onion, thinly sliced
  ½ cup fresh lemon juice
  2 teaspoons sugar (optional)
  1 teaspoon oregano
  1 teaspoon grated lemon peel
  1 small clove garlic, minced, or pinch garlic powder (optional)
    Salt and pepper to taste (optional)

Score steak ⅛-inch deep on both sides in diamond design with sharp knife. Place steak in baking dish or heavy-duty plastic bag. Combine remaining ingredients in bowl and pour over steak. Refrigerate, covered, several hours, turning steak several times. Remove steak from marinade; reserve marinade. Broil or grill steak 3 inches from heat, 4 to 6 minutes on each side, or until done as desired. Meanwhile, heat mushrooms and onion in reserved marinade in tightly covered skillet, 1 to 2 minutes. To serve, slice steak very thinly against the grain. Top with onion and mushrooms.

Makes 6 servings

	Per Serving
Calories	160
Carbohydrate (g)	3
Protein (g)	24
Total Fat (g)	6
Cholesterol (mg)	71
Sodium (mg)	45

MEXICAN STEAK

1 pound lean top round steak, trimmed of fat
1 cup no-salt-added tomato juice
1 large onion, thinly sliced
1 clove garlic, minced (optional)
1 teaspoon chili powder, or to taste
½ teaspoon oregano
  Pinch ground cumin (optional)
  Salt and pepper to taste (optional)

Spray large nonstick skillet with cooking spray. Add steak and brown quickly on both sides over high heat. Pour off any fat. Add remaining ingredients. Simmer uncovered until onions are tender and sauce is thick. Steak should be pink in the middle.

Makes 4 servings

	Per Serving
Calories	154
Carbohydrate (g)	6
Protein (g)	22
Total Fat (g)	4
Cholesterol (mg)	61
Sodium (mg)	65

SPICY INDIAN HAMBURGERS

1 pound lean beef round,
    trimmed of fat, ground
¼ cup low-fat plain yogurt
2 tablespoons minced onion
½ teaspoon ground cumin
½ teaspoon ground turmeric
¼ teaspoon ground ginger
⅛ teaspoon garlic powder
    Salt and pepper to taste
    (optional)

Mix all ingredients thoroughly in bowl. Shape into 4 patties. Broil or grill 4 inches from heat, about 5 minutes on each side, or until done as desired.

Makes 4 servings

	Per Serving
Calories	140
Carbohydrate (g)	2
Protein (g)	22
Total Fat (g)	4
Cholesterol (mg)	62
Sodium (mg)	62

APPLE BASTING SAUCE

½ cup unsweetened applesauce
½ cup dry white wine

Combine ingredients thoroughly in a bowl. (Use to baste meat during roasting.)

Makes 1 cup

	Per Tablespoon
Calories	4
Carbohydrate (g)	1
Protein (g)	0
Total Fat (g)	0
Cholesterol (mg)	0
Sodium (mg)	1

SPEEDY MOUSSAKA

1 pound lean beef round,
    trimmed of fat, ground
2 cups no-salt-added tomato
    sauce
1 small onion, minced
½ teaspoon garlic powder
½ teaspoon oregano
⅛ teaspoon ground cinnamon
⅛ teaspoon ground nutmeg
1 eggplant (about 1¼
    pounds), pared, diced
2 ounces part-skim feta
    cheese, crumbled
    (optional)

Break meat into chunks in baking pan. Broil meat until browned. Pour off fat. For sauce, combine tomato sauce, onion, garlic powder, oregano, cinnamon and nutmeg in bowl. Layer meat, sauce and eggplant in ovenproof casserole. Sprinkle with cheese, if desired. Bake in preheated 350°F oven 45 minutes.

Makes 4 servings

	Per Serving
Calories	206
Carbohydrate (g)	18
Protein (g)	24
Total Fat (g)	5
Cholesterol (mg)	61
Sodium (mg)	81

STEAK STROGANOFF

1½ pounds lean boneless round
    steak, trimmed of fat
1 tablespoon safflower or corn
    oil
½ pound fresh mushrooms,
    thinly sliced
1 onion, thinly sliced
    Salt and pepper to taste
    (optional)
1 tablespoon instant-blend
    flour
½ cup low-fat plain yogurt
¼ cup sherry

Cut steak into thin slices. Spray large nonstick skillet with cooking spray. Combine meat, oil, mushrooms, onion, salt and pepper in skillet. Cook over moderate heat until meat is well browned. Mix flour with yogurt in small cup until smooth; stir into meat mixture. Cook, stirring constantly, until thickened. Add sherry; simmer 3 minutes.

Makes 6 servings

	Per Serving
Calories	207
Carbohydrate (g)	6
Protein (g)	27
Total Fat (g)	8
Cholesterol (mg)	75
Sodium (mg)	101

SAVORY YANKEE CHUCK ROAST

3½ pounds lean boneless chuck
    arm roast, trimmed of fat
3 cups water
1 teaspoon savory
1 bay leaf
    Salt and pepper to taste
    (optional)

1 pound carrots, sliced
1 pound white turnips, pared,
    sliced
2 cups fresh or frozen small
    white onions
2 stalks celery, sliced
2 tablespoons instant-blend
    flour
¼ cup cold water

Brown meat on all sides under broiler. Place meat in Dutch oven; add 3 cups water, the savory, bay leaf, salt and pepper. Cover and simmer over very low heat 3 hours, or until meat is tender. Remove and discard bay leaf. Cool to room temperature. Refrigerate overnight. Remove and discard hardened fat. Heat to boiling. Stir in carrots, turnips, onions and celery. Cover and simmer over low heat 20 to 30 minutes, or until vegetables are tender. Remove meat to serving platter; remove vegetables with slotted spoon and place around meat. Keep warm. Combine flour and ¼ cup cold water in small cup until smooth; stir into simmering liquid. Cook, stirring constantly, until sauce is thick. Serve meat and vegetables with sauce.

Makes 12 servings

	Per Serving
Calories	242
Carbohydrate (g)	8
Protein (g)	29
Total Fat (g)	10
Cholesterol (mg)	86
Sodium (mg)	143

Savory Yankee Chuck Roast

ORIENTAL BEEF AND ASPARAGUS

2 teaspoons safflower or corn oil
1¼ pounds lean flank steak
1 pound fresh asparagus
2 large onions
¼ cup dry white wine
3 tablespoons low-sodium soy sauce
1 teaspoon cornstarch or arrowroot
½ teaspoon sugar (optional)

Spray large nonstick skillet with cooking spray. Heat oil in skillet. Add meat and brown quickly on both sides over high heat; remove from skillet. Slice against the grain into very thin strips; reserve. Break off tough bottom stems of asparagus and discard. Cut asparagus spears into 1-inch lengths. Cut onions into thick slices. Combine asparagus, onions and wine in skillet. Cook, covered, over moderately high heat 2 minutes. Separate onion slices into rings. Stir together soy sauce, cornstarch and sugar in small bowl and add to skillet. Cook and stir over moderate heat until liquid has reduced to a sauce. Stir in reserved steak strips. Cook only until heated through to desired doneness. Meat should be rare, and vegetables should be crisp-tender.

Makes 5 servings

	Per Serving
Calories	222
Carbohydrate (g)	8
Protein (g)	27
Total Fat (g)	9
Cholesterol (mg)	77
Sodium (mg)	453

LEMON-SEASONED STEAK

1½ pounds lean chuck steak, trimmed of fat
Juice of 1 lemon
1 clove garlic, minced
½ teaspoon crumbled savory, or other herbs to taste (optional)
Coarsely ground pepper

Moisten steak with lemon juice; sprinkle with garlic, herbs and pepper. Puncture repeatedly with fork. Cover with plastic wrap or waxed paper. Let stand 30 minutes at room temperature or several hours in refrigerator. (If refrigerated, allow to reach room temperature before broiling.) Broil or grill 4 inches from heat, turning once, until done as desired. Best if served rare or medium-rare.

Makes 6 servings

	Per Serving
Calories	186
Carbohydrate (g)	1
Protein (g)	26
Total Fat (g)	8
Cholesterol (mg)	78
Sodium (mg)	45

Oriental Beef and Asparagus

MEXICAN STUFFED GREEN PEPPERS

8 large green bell peppers
  Boiling water
2 pounds lean beef round,
  trimmed of fat, ground
1 can (6 ounces) tomato paste
2 cloves garlic, minced
1 to 2 tablespoons chili
  powder
  Salt and pepper to taste
  (optional)
8 teaspoons Italian-seasoned
  bread crumbs

Cut a thin slice from stem ends of peppers; discard ends. Remove and discard seeds and white pulp. Cook peppers in boiling water to cover 5 minutes. Drain. Spray large nonstick skillet with cooking spray. Brown meat in skillet over moderate heat. Pour off fat. Break meat into chunks. Add tomato paste, garlic, chili powder and salt and pepper, if desired. Cook over low heat 5 minutes. Spoon meat mixture into peppers. Sprinkle tops with bread crumbs. Place in shallow baking pan and add ½ inch water. Bake in a preheated 350°F oven 30 minutes.

Makes 8 servings

Per Serving	
Calories	211
Carbohydrate (g)	12
Protein (g)	27
Total Fat (g)	6
Cholesterol (mg)	74
Sodium (mg)	337

HAMBURGER SAUERBRATEN

1½ pounds lean beef round,
  trimmed of fat, ground
¼ cup liquid egg substitute
2 tablespoons minced onion
  Salt and pepper to taste
  (optional)
  Pinch thyme
1 cup cold water
1 tablespoon instant-blend
  flour
2 tablespoons no-salt-added
  catsup
1 tablespoon brown sugar
1 tablespoon cider vinegar
1 bay leaf
¼ teaspoon ground ginger
¼ teaspoon ground cloves

Mix meat, egg substitute, onion, salt and pepper thoroughly in a bowl. Shape into 6 patties. Spray large nonstick skillet with cooking spray. Brown burgers in skillet quickly on both sides over high heat. Remove burgers to platter. Pour off any fat. Mix water with flour in small cup until smooth; add to skillet. Stir in remaining ingredients. Heat to boiling, stirring constantly. Reduce heat; add burgers. Simmer, uncovered, 20 minutes.

Makes 6 servings

Per Serving	
Calories	156
Carbohydrate (g)	6
Protein (g)	23
Total Fat (g)	4
Cholesterol (mg)	61
Sodium (mg)	134

Mexican Stuffed Green Peppers

SKILLET-BARBECUED STEAKS

8 minute steaks (cubed round
  steaks), ¼ pound each
1 cup low-sodium tomato
  sauce
½ cup chopped green bell
  pepper
¼ cup unsweetened pineapple
  juice
2 tablespoons instant minced
  onion
1 tablespoon Worcestershire
  sauce
1 tablespoon prepared
  mustard
2 or 3 drops smoke seasoning
  (optional)
  Salt and pepper to taste
  (optional)

Spray large nonstick skillet with
cooking spray. Brown steaks on
both sides in skillet. Pour off any
fat. Stir in remaining ingredients.
Cook and stir, uncovered, until
sauce is thick.

Makes 8 servings

	Per Serving
Calories	149
Carbohydrate (g)	5
Protein (g)	22
Total Fat (g)	4
Cholesterol (mg)	61
Sodium (mg)	103

RED WINE ROUND ROAST

3½ pounds lean bottom round
  roast, trimmed of fat,
  boned and tied
½ teaspoon poultry seasoning
½ teaspoon pumpkin pie spice
1 clove garlic, minced
  Salt and pepper to taste
  (optional)
½ cup dry red table wine
½ cup water
1 bay leaf
2 cups fresh or frozen small
  white onions
2 cups sliced fresh
  mushrooms
2 tablespoons instant-blend
  flour
¼ cup cold water

Brown meat on all sides under
broiler. Transfer meat to heavy
Dutch oven. Sprinkle with
seasonings; add wine, ½ cup
water and bay leaf. Cover and
simmer over low heat 3 hours, or
until meat is very tender. Drain
pan juices into heat-resistant
container; skim surface fat
carefully with bulb-type baster.
Return fat-skimmed broth to pot.
Stir in vegetables. Cover and
simmer until onions are tender, 10
to 20 minutes. Remove meat to
serving platter. Remove
vegetables with slotted spoon and
place around meat. Keep warm.
Mix flour and ¼ cup cold water in
small cup until smooth; stir into
simmering liquid. Cook, stirring
constantly, until sauce thickens
and bubbles. Remove bay leaf.
Serve meat and vegetables with
sauce.

Makes 12 servings

	Per Serving
Calories	165
Carbohydrate (g)	5
Protein (g)	24
Total Fat (g)	5
Cholesterol (mg)	69
Sodium (mg)	62

STEAK AND PEPPERS

2 pounds lean round steak, trimmed of fat
1 tablespoon safflower or corn oil
1 can (28 ounces) no-salt-added tomatoes, drained, chopped
2 medium onions, sliced
¼ cup Chianti or other dry red wine
1 clove garlic, minced
½ teaspoon basil
Salt and pepper to taste (optional)
2 red or green bell peppers (or 1 of each), cut into strips

Cut meat into 8 equal pieces. Spray large nonstick skillet with cooking spray. Heat oil in skillet. Add meat and brown quickly over high heat. Pour off fat. Stir in remaining ingredients except pepper strips. Reduce heat. Simmer covered until meat is tender, 1 hour or more. Add pepper strips. Simmer uncovered until pepper is tender and liquid has reduced to a thick sauce.

Makes 8 servings

Per Serving	
Calories	177
Carbohydrate (g)	8
Protein (g)	22
Total Fat (g)	6
Cholesterol (mg)	61
Sodium (mg)	66

CURRIED LAMB CHOPS AND APRICOTS

6 lean loin lamb chops, ¾-inch thick, trimmed of fat
1 cup fat-skimmed chicken broth, low-sodium canned or homemade
½ cup chopped onion
¼ cup all-purpose flour
1 teaspoon curry powder
1 teaspoon ground turmeric
¼ teaspoon pepper
1 cup skim milk
1 can (16 ounces) juice-packed unpeeled apricot halves, drained

Spray large nonstick skillet with cooking spray. Brown chops well on both sides over moderately high heat. Remove chops from skillet. Pour off fat. Heat broth in same skillet. Add onion; cook and stir over low heat to get up any brown particles from bottom of skillet. Continue to cook over moderately low heat, stirring frequently. Combine flour, curry powder, turmeric and pepper in small bowl; mix in milk gradually. Stir slowly into chicken broth. Cook, stirring constantly, until thickened; boil 1 minute. Place chops in single layer in baking dish. Add apricots; pour on sauce. Bake in a preheated 350°F oven about 1 hour, or until chops are tender.

Makes 6 servings

Per Serving	
Calories	207
Carbohydrate (g)	18
Protein (g)	21
Total Fat (g)	5
Cholesterol (mg)	66
Sodium (mg)	79

SOUVLAKI-STYLE LAMBURGER

1 pound lamb (from leg),
    trimmed of fat, ground
1 clove garlic, minced
1 teaspoon oregano
1 teaspoon dried mint leaves
¼ teaspoon ground nutmeg
¼ teaspoon ground cinnamon
    Salt and pepper to taste
    (optional)
1 can (16 ounces) no-salt-
    added tomatoes, cut up
1 onion, chopped
1 small or ½ medium
    cucumber, pared, diced
1⅓ cups cooked rice (optional)
¼ cup low-fat plain yogurt
    (optional)

Spray large nonstick skillet with cooking spray. Spread lamb in skillet; sprinkle with garlic, oregano, mint, nutmeg, cinnamon, salt and pepper. Cook over moderate heat until underside is browned. Break up with fork into bite-size chunks. Continue to cook and stir until chunks are well browned. Pour off fat. Add tomatoes and onion. Simmer uncovered, stirring frequently, until nearly all the liquid has evaporated. Stir in cucumber and heat through. (Serve over rice and top with chilled yogurt, if desired.)
Makes 4 servings

	Per Serving
Calories	192
Carbohydrate (g)	8
Protein (g)	24
Total Fat (g)	7
Cholesterol (mg)	79
Sodium (mg)	266

GREEK BROILED LAMB CHOPS

4 lean loin lamb chops,
    ¾-inch thick, trimmed of
    fat
2 tablespoons fresh lemon
    juice
1 tablespoon dried mint
    leaves, crushed
⅛ teaspoon ground cinnamon
⅛ teaspoon ground nutmeg
1 clove garlic, minced
    (optional)
    Salt and pepper to taste
    (optional)
    Fresh mint sprigs (optional)
    Lemon slices (optional)

Sprinkle chops with lemon juice and seasonings; puncture repeatedly with a fork. Wrap in plastic; refrigerate several hours. Broil or grill chops 4 to 5 inches from heat, turning once, until brown and crisp outside but still pink in center or until done as desired. Garnish with fresh mint sprigs and lemon slices, if desired.
Makes 4 servings

	Per Serving
Calories	118
Carbohydrate (g)	1
Protein (g)	17
Total Fat (g)	5
Cholesterol (mg)	61
Sodium (mg)	44

Greek Broiled Lamb Chops

PINEAPPLE PORK ROAST

5 pounds fat-trimmed, rolled pork roast
2 cups canned unsweetened pineapple juice
1 can (8 ounces) juice-packed crushed pineapple, undrained
½ cup chopped onion
½ cup sliced celery
¼ cup golden raisins
¼ cup cider vinegar
¼ cup low-sodium soy sauce (optional)
½ teaspoon ground ginger
¼ cup cornstarch
Cold water

Place pork in roasting pan. Mix together remaining ingredients, except cornstarch and cold water, in a bowl. Spoon pineapple mixture over pork. Bake covered in a preheated 325°F oven about 3 hours, or until tender, basting frequently with pineapple mixture. Remove meat to heated platter; keep warm. Skim any fat from pan drippings. Mix cornstarch with enough cold water in a small cup to make a thin paste. Stir into pan juices. Cook over moderate heat, stirring constantly, until gravy thickens. Pour over roast.

Makes 16 servings

	Per Serving
Calories	254
Carbohydrate (g)	9
Protein (g)	28
Total Fat (g)	11
Cholesterol (mg)	95
Sodium (mg)	112

BAKED PORK CHOPS OREGANO

6 lean center-cut pork chops (about 2¼ pounds), trimmed of fat
Salt and pepper to taste (optional)
1 tablespoon water
1 pound fresh mushrooms, sliced
2 cups chopped canned no-salt-added tomatoes
2 green bell peppers, chopped
2 onions, sliced
2 teaspoons oregano
1 clove garlic, minced (optional)

Spray large nonstick skillet with cooking spray. Sprinkle chops with salt and pepper, if desired. Place chops and the water in skillet. Simmer uncovered until water has evaporated and chops begin to brown. Brown quickly on both sides. Arrange chops in single layer in shallow baking pan. Combine remaining ingredients in bowl and arrange over chops. Cover pan with foil. Bake in preheated 325°F oven for 1 hour. Remove foil and continue to bake 20 to 30 minutes, or until chops are very tender.

Makes 6 servings

	Per Serving
Calories	229
Carbohydrate (g)	11
Protein (g)	27
Total Fat (g)	9
Cholesterol (mg)	70
Sodium (mg)	208

Pineapple Pork Roast

CHILLED SHRIMP AND MUSHROOM KEBABS

	Per Serving
Calories	177
Carbohydrate (g)	7
Protein (g)	20
Total Fat (g)	8
Cholesterol (mg)	114
Sodium (mg)	117

½ pound fresh whole
  mushrooms, stems
  removed
1 cucumber, pared, quartered,
  cut into chunks
1 pound cooked, shelled,
  deveined shrimp
3 tablespoons safflower or
  corn oil
2 tablespoons white or cider
  vinegar
1 small onion, finely chopped
2 tablespoons fresh lemon
  juice
2 tablespoons water
1 tablespoon prepared
  horseradish
  Salt and pepper to taste
  (optional)
½ teaspoon garlic powder
¼ teaspoon tarragon, or to
  taste
24 cherry tomatoes

Place mushroom caps in bowl
with cucumber chunks and
shrimp. Beat oil with vinegar,
onion, lemon juice, water,
horseradish, salt, pepper, garlic
powder and tarragon in small
bowl. Pour over mushrooms,
shrimp and cucumber; stir to mix
well. Cover and refrigerate several
hours or overnight. Drain shrimp,
mushrooms and cucumber.
Thread tomatoes, mushrooms,
shrimp and cucumber alternately
on skewers, dividing evenly
among 12 skewers.
Makes 6 servings

KEY LIME MULLET

2 pounds mullet fillets or other
  fish fillets
  Salt and pepper to taste
  (optional)
¼ cup fresh lime juice
3 tablespoons diet margarine,
  melted
  Paprika
  Lime wedges (optional)

Cut fillets into serving-size
pieces. Place in single layer in
shallow baking dish. Sprinkle with
salt and pepper, if desired. Pour
lime juice over fish; cover and
refrigerate for 30 minutes, turning
once. Remove fish, reserving
juice. Place fish on broiler pan
sprayed with cooking spray.
Combine reserved juice with
margarine in a small cup. Brush
fish with juice mixture and
sprinkle with paprika. Broil about
4 inches from heat source for 8 to
10 minutes or until fish flakes
easily when tested with a fork.
Serve with lime wedges, if desired.
Makes 8 servings

	Per Serving
Calories	186
Carbohydrate (g)	1
Protein (g)	22
Total Fat (g)	10
Cholesterol (mg)	62
Sodium (mg)	144

Chilled Shrimp and Mushroom Kebabs

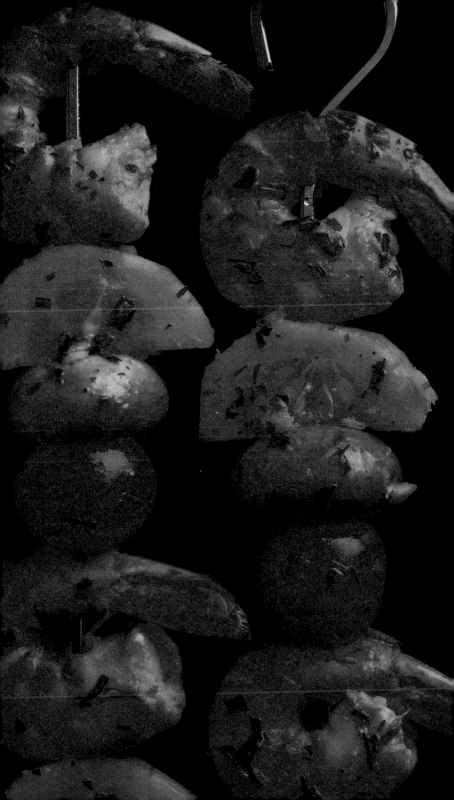

SALMON PAYSANNE

2 pounds salmon steaks or
   other fish steaks
Salt and pepper to taste
   (optional)
1 can (4 ounces) sliced
   mushrooms, drained
½ cup sliced green onions
¼ cup no-salt-added catsup
½ teaspoon liquid smoke
   seasoning (optional)

Place steaks in single layer in
nonstick baking dish sprayed with
cooking spray. Sprinkle with salt
and pepper, if desired. Combine
remaining ingredients in a bowl.
Spoon mixture onto steaks,
dividing evenly. Bake in preheated
350°F oven for 25 to 30 minutes
or until fish flakes easily when
tested with a fork.

Makes 8 servings

	Per Serving
Calories	254
Carbohydrate (g)	1
Protein (g)	26
Total Fat (g)	15
Cholesterol (mg)	44
Sodium (mg)	142

ITALIAN FISH STEW

1 teaspoon safflower or corn
   oil
2 tablespoons water
1 cup chopped onion
1 clove garlic, minced
   (optional)
1 can (16 ounces) no-salt-
   added tomatoes,
   undrained, cut up
1 green bell pepper, diced
2 stalks celery, diced
3 tablespoons chopped fresh
   Italian parsley
3 tablespoons dry white wine
1 small bay leaf
Salt and pepper to taste
   (optional)
1 teaspoon oregano
1 teaspoon fennel seeds
1 pound frozen cod fillets,
   slightly thawed

Spray large nonstick skillet with
cooking spray. Add oil, water,
onion and garlic, if desired. Cook,
stirring frequently, until water
evaporates and onions are lightly
browned. Add remaining
ingredients except fish. Cover and
simmer 25 to 30 minutes. Cut
fillets into 1½-inch chunks. Add
to skillet. Cover and simmer 12 to
15 minutes or until fish flakes
easily when tested with fork.
Remove bay leaf before serving.

Makes 4 servings

	Per Serving
Calories	150
Carbohydrate (g)	11
Protein (g)	22
Total Fat (g)	2
Cholesterol (mg)	57
Sodium (mg)	115

QUICK SEAFOOD NEWBURG

1 cup skim milk
2 tablespoons instant-blend
  flour
¼ cup sherry
  Salt and black pepper to
    taste (optional)
  Pinch ground nutmeg
  Pinch cayenne pepper
2 cups cold cooked, shelled
  lobster or shrimp, or 2
  cans (7 ounces each) low-
  sodium water-packed tuna
4 slices toasted high-fiber
  bread, cut into halves
  diagonally
2 tablespoons minced fresh
  parsley
  Paprika
  Lemon wedges (optional)

Stir milk and flour together in
saucepan until smooth. Cook and
stir over low heat until sauce
simmers and thickens. Stir in
sherry, salt, black pepper, nutmeg,
cayenne pepper and seafood.
Cook and stir until heated
through. Spoon over toast
triangles and sprinkle with parsley
and paprika. Garnish with lemon
wedges, if desired.

Makes 4 servings

	Per Serving
Calories	163
Carbohydrate (g)	17
Protein (g)	19
Total Fat (g)	2
Cholesterol (mg)	63
Sodium (mg)	344

CUCUMBER SAUCE

1 cup finely diced cucumber
1 onion, chopped
¼ cup reduced-calorie
  mayonnaise
¼ cup low-fat plain yogurt
½ teaspoon celery seeds

Combine all ingredients
thoroughly in a bowl. Serve with
hot or cold seafood.

Makes 1 cup

	Per Tablespoon
Calories	15
Carbohydrate (g)	1
Protein (g)	0
Total Fat (g)	1
Cholesterol (mg)	1
Sodium (mg)	31

DILL SAUCE

¼ cup low-fat plain yogurt
2 tablespoons fresh dillweed,
  minced
½ cup reduced-calorie
  mayonnaise

Combine all ingredients
thoroughly in a bowl. Serve with
cold seafood.

Makes ¾ cup

	Per Tablespoon
Calories	31
Carbohydrate (g)	1
Protein (g)	0
Total Fat (g)	3
Cholesterol (mg)	4
Sodium (mg)	79

COD CREOLE

1 tablespoon diet margarine
½ cup chopped onion
½ cup chopped green bell
  pepper
¼ pound fresh mushrooms,
  sliced
1 can (16 ounces) no-salt-
  added tomatoes,
  undrained, chopped
1 tablespoon fresh lemon juice
⅛ teaspoon dry mustard
1 bay leaf
¼ teaspoon red pepper sauce
  (optional)
  Salt and pepper to taste
  (optional)
1 pound cod fillets

Melt margarine in large nonstick
skillet. Add onion and green
pepper; sauté until tender. Add
mushrooms; cook 3 minutes. Add
tomatoes, lemon juice, mustard,
bay leaf, red pepper sauce, salt
and pepper. Simmer covered 15
minutes. Cut cod fillets into
serving-size pieces; add to skillet.
Cover and simmer 8 to 10
minutes or until fish flakes easily
when tested with a fork.

Makes 4 servings

	Per Serving
Calories	142
Carbohydrate (g)	9
Protein (g)	22
Total Fat (g)	2
Cholesterol (mg)	57
Sodium (mg)	131

HEARTY HALIBUT

2 pounds halibut steaks or
  other fish steaks
⅔ cup thinly sliced onion
1½ cups chopped fresh
  mushrooms
⅓ cup chopped tomato
¼ cup chopped green bell
  pepper
¼ cup chopped fresh parsley
3 tablespoons chopped
  pimiento
½ cup dry white wine
2 tablespoons fresh lemon
  juice
¼ teaspoon dillweed
⅛ teaspoon pepper
  Lemon wedges (optional)

Cut steaks into serving-size
pieces. Spray baking dish with
cooking spray. Arrange onion over
bottom of dish. Place fish in single
layer over onion. Combine
mushrooms, tomato, green
pepper, parsley and pimiento in a
bowl; spread over top of fish.
Combine wine, lemon juice and
seasonings in a bowl; pour over
vegetables. Bake in preheated
350°F oven for 25 to 30
minutes or until fish flakes easily
when tested with a fork. Serve
with lemon wedges, if desired.

Makes 8 servings

	Per Serving
Calories	129
Carbohydrate (g)	3
Protein (g)	24
Total Fat (g)	1
Cholesterol (mg)	57
Sodium (mg)	66

STRIPED BASS WITH STUFFING

3 pounds dressed striped bass or other dressed fish
Low-Cal Stuffing (recipe follows)
1 tablespoon safflower or corn oil
Lemon wedges (optional)

Clean, wash and dry fish. Prepare Low-Cal Stuffing; stuff fish loosely with stuffing. Close opening with small skewers or wooden picks. Place fish in nonstick baking dish sprayed with cooking spray; brush fish with oil. Bake in preheated 350°F oven for 40 to 60 minutes or until fish flakes easily when tested with a fork. Remove skewers. Serve with lemon wedges, if desired.

NOTE: If all stuffing will not fit into cavity of fish, place remainder in covered casserole; bake separately. Serve with fish.

Makes 6 servings

	Per Serving
Calories	221
Carbohydrate (g)	8
Protein (g)	27
Total Fat (g)	9
Cholesterol (mg)	77
Sodium (mg)	104

LOW-CAL STUFFING

1 tablespoon safflower or corn oil
¾ cup chopped onion
2¼ cups pared, chopped apple
⅓ cup chopped celery
⅓ cup chopped fresh parsley
2 tablespoons fresh lemon juice
⅛ teaspoon thyme

Heat oil in nonstick skillet sprayed with cooking spray. Add onion to skillet; sauté until tender. Combine onion with remaining ingredients; mix thoroughly.

Makes about 3 cups

	Per ½ Cup
Calories	54
Carbohydrate (g)	8
Protein (g)	0
Total Fat (g)	2
Cholesterol (mg)	0
Sodium (mg)	9

OVEN-FRIED FISH FILLETS

1 pound flounder fillets or other fish fillets
2 tablespoons reduced-calorie mayonnaise
5 tablespoons fine dry bread crumbs
1 teaspoon parsley flakes
½ teaspoon paprika

Cut fillets into serving-size pieces. Coat with mayonnaise on both sides. Mix crumbs, parsley and paprika in shallow dish. Press fillets into crumb mixture to coat both sides. Place on nonstick baking sheet. Bake in preheated 450°F oven 12 minutes or until fish flakes easily when tested with a fork.

Makes 4 servings

	Per Serving
Calories	141
Carbohydrate (g)	6
Protein (g)	20
Total Fat (g)	3
Cholesterol (mg)	60
Sodium (mg)	202

Striped Bass with Stuffing

ORANGE-SPIKED ZUCCHINI AND CARROTS

1 pound zucchini, cut into
   ¼-inch slices
1 package (10 ounces) frozen
   sliced carrots, thawed
1 cup unsweetened orange
   juice
1 stalk celery, finely chopped
2 tablespoons chopped onion
   Salt and pepper to taste
   (optional)

Combine all ingredients in nonstick saucepan. Cover and simmer 10 to 12 minutes, or until zucchini is tender. Uncover and simmer until most of liquid has evaporated.

Makes 7 servings

	Per Serving
Calories	43
Carbohydrate (g)	10
Protein (g)	1
Total Fat (g)	0
Cholesterol (mg)	0
Sodium (mg)	31

VEGETABLES

RED CABBAGE WITH APPLES

**1 small head red cabbage
(about 1 pound), shredded
2 large apples, pared, thinly
sliced
½ cup unsweetened apple juice
¼ cup fresh lemon juice
1 onion, sliced
2 tablespoons raisins
2 tablespoons brown sugar
Salt and pepper to taste
(optional)**

Toss all ingredients together in
nonstick saucepan. Cover and
simmer 30 minutes, or until
cabbage is tender.

Makes 8 servings

	Per Serving
Calories	69
Carbohydrate (g)	17
Protein (g)	1
Total Fat (g)	0
Cholesterol (mg)	0
Sodium (mg)	10

CIDER-PICKLED GREEN BEANS

**1 pound sliced fresh green
beans
1 small onion, sliced,
separated into rings
½ cup thawed, undiluted frozen
unsweetened apple juice
or cider concentrate
½ cup cider vinegar
½ cup boiling water
1 teaspoon celery seed
¼ teaspoon dill seed
Pinch ground turmeric**

Combine all ingredients in non-
aluminum saucepan. Simmer until
beans are just tender. Cool. Cover
and refrigerate at least 12 hours
before serving.   *Makes 6 servings*

	Per Serving
Calories	69
Carbohydrate (g)	17
Protein (g)	2
Total Fat (g)	0
Cholesterol (mg)	0
Sodium (mg)	11

HAWAIIAN CARROTS

**2 cups fresh or frozen sliced
carrots
1 cup fat-skimmed chicken
broth, low-sodium canned
or homemade
¼ cup minced onion
¼ cup chopped green bell
pepper
1 can (8 ounces) juice-packed
pineapple chunks, drained,
juice reserved
2 teaspoons cornstarch or
arrowroot**

Place carrots and chicken broth
in saucepan. Cover and simmer
10 minutes, or until carrots are
nearly tender. Add onion and
green pepper. Cook, uncovered, 2
minutes. Drain liquid from
saucepan. Add pineapple. Cook 1
minute. Mix cornstarch with
reserved pineapple juice in a small
bowl until well blended; stir into
simmering vegetables. Cook and
stir until mixture simmers and
thickens.

Makes 6 servings

	Per Serving
Calories	50
Carbohydrate (g)	11
Protein (g)	1
Total Fat (g)	0
Cholesterol (mg)	0
Sodium (mg)	35

Red Cabbage with Apples

BRUSSELS SPROUTS IN ORANGE SAUCE

4 cups fresh Brussels sprouts
1 can (6 ounces) unsweetened orange juice
½ cup water
½ teaspoon cornstarch
¼ teaspoon ground cinnamon
Salt and pepper to taste (optional)

Combine all ingredients in saucepan. Cover and simmer 6 to 7 minutes or until Brussels sprouts are nearly tender. Uncover and continue to simmer, stirring occasionally, until most of the liquid has evaporated.

Makes 6 servings

	Per Serving
Calories	39
Carbohydrate (g)	9
Protein (g)	2
Total Fat (g)	0
Cholesterol (mg)	0
Sodium (mg)	15

CONFETTI CABBAGE

1 onion, chopped
1 tablespoon diet margarine
3 cups shredded cabbage
1 cup shredded carrots
½ cup water
½ teaspoon oregano
⅛ teaspoon garlic powder
Salt and pepper to taste (optional)

Sauté onion in margarine in large skillet until just transparent. Stir in remaining ingredients. Cover and cook over moderate heat 5 minutes. Uncover and simmer until most of the liquid has evaporated and cabbage is tender.

Makes 4 servings

	Per Serving
Calories	44
Carbohydrate (g)	7
Protein (g)	1
Total Fat (g)	2
Cholesterol (mg)	0
Sodium (mg)	54

CREOLE CORN

1 can (16 ounces) no-salt-added stewed tomatoes, undrained, cut up
1 small green bell pepper, chopped
1 onion, chopped
1 stalk celery, chopped
2 cups fresh or thawed frozen whole-kernel corn
Salt and pepper to taste (optional)

Simmer tomatoes, green pepper, onion and celery in nonstick saucepan 20 minutes. Stir in corn and salt and pepper, if desired. Cook 5 minutes, or until corn is tender.

Makes 8 servings

	Per Serving
Calories	57
Carbohydrate (g)	13
Protein (g)	2
Total Fat (g)	1
Cholesterol (mg)	0
Sodium (mg)	16

MASHED SQUASH

1 medium acorn squash, halved, seeded
1 tablespoon maple syrup
½ teaspoon pumpkin pie spice
Pepper to taste (optional)

Place squash halves, cut-sides down, on baking sheet. Bake in preheated 400°F oven 30 minutes, or until tender. Scoop out squash into mixing bowl; beat with electric mixer. Stir in syrup, pumpkin pie spice and pepper.

Makes 4 servings

Per Serving	
Calories	56
Carbohydrate (g)	15
Protein (g)	1
Total Fat (g)	0
Cholesterol (mg)	0
Sodium (mg)	4

MARINATED MUSHROOMS

1 pound fresh mushrooms, sliced
¼ cup water
¼ cup fresh lemon juice
1 tablespoon safflower or corn oil
2 teaspoons oregano
1 teaspoon grated lemon rind
1 clove garlic, minced
   Salt and pepper to taste (optional)

Combine all ingredients in glass bowl or plastic bag. Cover and refrigerate, stirring occasionally, 8 hours or overnight. Drain mushrooms before serving.

Makes 6 servings

Per Serving	
Calories	44
Carbohydrate (g)	5
Protein (g)	2
Total Fat (g)	3
Cholesterol (mg)	0
Sodium (mg)	3

LOW-CALORIE CREAM SAUCE

1 can (13 ounces) evaporated skim milk
¼ cup instant-blend flour
1 teaspoon chopped fresh parsley
Pinch ground nutmeg
Pinch white pepper

Stir milk and flour in nonstick saucepan until smooth. Cook and stir over very low heat until sauce begins to bubble; simmer 2 minutes. Stir in remaining ingredients. (Increase or decrease amount of flour for thicker or thinner sauce.)

Makes 1⅓ cups

Per Tablespoon	
Calories	22
Carbohydrate (g)	4
Protein (g)	1
Total Fat (g)	0
Cholesterol (mg)	1
Sodium (mg)	24

ORIENTAL STIR-FRIED BOK CHOY

1 tablespoon safflower or corn oil
1 clove garlic, minced
1 large head bok choy (celery cabbage), cut into large chunks
1 tablespoon low-sodium soy sauce
1 tablespoon dry white wine

Heat oil in wok or large nonstick skillet. Sauté garlic until brown. Add bok choy; sprinkle with soy sauce and wine. Cook and stir over high heat 1 minute. Serve immediately.

Makes 6 servings

Per Serving	
Calories	43
Carbohydrate (g)	4
Protein (g)	2
Total Fat (g)	3
Cholesterol (mg)	0
Sodium (mg)	200

STIR-FRIED PEPPERS AND ONIONS

2 red or green bell peppers (or 1 of each), cut into narrow strips
1 large Spanish onion, sliced
2 tablespoons low-sodium soy sauce (optional)
2 tablespoons white wine
2 teaspoons safflower or corn oil

Combine all ingredients in nonstick skillet. Cover and simmer over moderate heat 2 minutes. Uncover and continue to cook, stirring frequently, until most of the liquid has evaporated and vegetables just begin to brown slightly.   *Makes 4 servings*

Per Serving	
Calories	47
Carbohydrate (g)	6
Protein (g)	1
Total Fat (g)	3
Cholesterol (mg)	0
Sodium (mg)	3

BROCCOLI SUPREME

1 package (10 ounces) frozen chopped broccoli
½ cup fat-skimmed chicken broth, low-sodium canned or homemade
3 tablespoons reduced-calorie mayonnaise
2 teaspoons instant minced onion (optional)

Place broccoli in saucepan. Stir remaining ingredients together in a bowl; add to broccoli. Cover and simmer, stirring occasionally, until broccoli is thawed. Uncover and continue to simmer, stirring occasionally, until most of liquid has evaporated and broccoli is tender.   *Makes 3 servings*

Per Serving	
Calories	69
Carbohydrate (g)	6
Protein (g)	3
Total Fat (g)	4
Cholesterol (mg)	5
Sodium (mg)	144

SKILLET GREEN BEANS AMANDINE

1 tablespoon slivered blanched almonds
1 pound fresh green beans or 1 package (10 ounces) frozen whole green beans, thawed
¼ cup fat-skimmed chicken broth, low-sodium canned or homemade
Salt and pepper to taste (optional)

Spread almonds in nonstick skillet. Shake skillet gently over moderate heat until almonds are toasted. Remove almonds; reserve. Combine green beans and chicken broth in the skillet. Simmer, uncovered, until most of the liquid has evaporated and beans are crisp-tender. Sprinkle with reserved almonds, and salt and pepper, if desired.   *Makes 3 servings*

Per Serving	
Calories	65
Carbohydrate (g)	11
Protein (g)	4
Total Fat (g)	2
Cholesterol (mg)	0
Sodium (mg)	14

HOT GERMAN POTATO SALAD

2 tablespoons safflower or
corn oil
⅓ cup finely chopped onion
1 tablespoon instant-blend
flour
¼ teaspoon dry mustard
¼ cup water
3 tablespoons cider vinegar
½ cup diced celery
3 tablespoons pickle relish
3 tablespoons chopped green
bell pepper
2½ cups diced cooked pared
potatoes

Heat oil in nonstick skillet. Add
onion; brown lightly. Combine
flour, mustard, water and vinegar
in small bowl; stir mixture into
onion. Cook over low heat until
sauce thickens. Combine celery,
pickle relish, pepper and potatoes
in large bowl. Add hot dressing;
mix lightly but thoroughly. Turn
into baking dish. Bake covered in
preheated 350°F oven about 20
minutes, or until heated.

Makes 6 servings

	Per Serving
Calories	118
Carbohydrate (g)	18
Protein (g)	1
Total Fat (g)	5
Cholesterol (mg)	0
Sodium (mg)	67

PASTA, POTATOES & RICE

MACARONI APPLE SALAD

2 cups tender-cooked protein-enriched elbow macaroni, rinsed, drained, chilled
2 red apples, diced
1 cup diced celery
¼ cup reduced-calorie mayonnaise
¼ cup low-fat plain yogurt
4 large lettuce leaves
¼ cup chopped walnuts

Combine macaroni, apples, celery, mayonnaise and yogurt in medium bowl; cover and chill. Serve on lettuce leaves; garnish with nuts.   *Makes 4 servings*

	Per Serving
Calories	223
Carbohydrate (g)	31
Protein (g)	5
Total Fat (g)	9
Cholesterol (mg)	6
Sodium (mg)	151

NOODLE LASAGNA

4 ounces uncooked wide egg noodles
1 cup low-fat cottage cheese
1 pound lean beef round, trimmed of fat, ground
1 can (28 ounces) no-salt-added tomatoes, undrained, well broken up
1 can (6 ounces) tomato paste
1 onion, chopped
1 clove garlic
2 teaspoons oregano
1 cup shredded part-skim mozzarella cheese
¼ cup grated Parmesan cheese

Cook noodles according to package directions. Rinse under cold water; drain. Combine with cottage cheese in medium bowl. Spray large nonstick skillet with cooking spray. Brown meat in skillet. Pour off fat. Stir in tomatoes, tomato paste, onion, garlic and oregano. Cover and simmer about 1½ hours, stirring occasionally. Pour ⅓ of the sauce into casserole; top with half the noodle mixture, then half the mozzarella cheese. Repeat layers; top with remaining sauce. Sprinkle with Parmesan. Bake in preheated 325°F oven 1 hour.

Makes 8 servings

	Per Serving
Calories	242
Carbohydrate (g)	21
Protein (g)	24
Total Fat (g)	7
Cholesterol (mg)	62
Sodium (mg)	452

APPLE-CURRY RICE

½ cup no-salt-added tomato juice
½ cup unsweetened apple juice
1 cup instant rice
1 teaspoon curry powder
1 red apple, unpared, diced

Combine all ingredients except apple in saucepan. Heat to boiling. Remove from heat; stir in apple. Cover tightly; let stand 5 minutes.

Makes 6 servings

	Per Serving
Calories	84
Carbohydrate (g)	19
Protein (g)	1
Total Fat (g)	0
Cholesterol (mg)	0
Sodium (mg)	3

Macaroni Apple Salad (top),
Noodle Lasagna (bottom)

QUICK SPANISH RICE

1 large onion, finely chopped
1 stalk celery, finely chopped
1 red or green bell pepper,
    diced
1 can (8 ounces) no-salt-added
    tomato sauce
1 can (8 ounces) no-salt-added
    tomatoes, well broken up
1¼ cups fat-skimmed chicken,
    turkey or beef broth, low-
    sodium canned or
    homemade
1 teaspoon prepared mustard
1 bay leaf
½ teaspoon oregano
2 cups instant rice

Combine all ingredients except rice in nonstick saucepan. Cover and simmer 10 minutes. Stir in rice. Simmer, covered, over very low heat, stirring occasionally, about 5 minutes.

Makes 8 servings

	Per Serving
Calories	114
Carbohydrate (g)	24
Protein (g)	3
Total Fat (g)	0
Cholesterol (mg)	0
Sodium (mg)	32

CREAMY STUFFED BAKED POTATOES

3 large baking potatoes
¾ cup low-fat plain yogurt
¼ cup reduced-calorie blue
    cheese salad dressing
1 tablespoon grated onion

Bake potatoes 1 hour in preheated 400°F oven. After removing potatoes, increase oven temperature setting to 450°F. Slice potatoes lengthwise in half. Scoop out potato; reserve shells. Combine potato, yogurt, salad dressing and onion in medium bowl; beat until fluffy. Divide among reserved shells. Place filled potato shells on baking sheet and return to oven. Bake at 450°F for 12 to 15 minutes.

Makes 6 servings

	Per Serving
Calories	83
Carbohydrate (g)	15
Protein (g)	4
Total Fat (g)	1
Cholesterol (mg)	2
Sodium (mg)	110

ALFIE'S FETTUCINE

8 ounces uncooked wide egg
    noodles
1 cup low-fat cottage cheese,
    at room temperature
½ cup grated Parmesan cheese
¼ cup minced fresh parsley
    Salt and coarsely ground
    pepper to taste (optional)

Boil noodles according to package directions. Drain and return to same pot. Quickly toss together with remaining ingredients. Serve immediately.

Makes 8 servings

	Per Serving
Calories	154
Carbohydrate (g)	21
Protein (g)	9
Total Fat (g)	3
Cholesterol (mg)	32
Sodium (mg)	210

Quick Spanish Rice

BANANA-RASPBERRY LAYER CAKE

½ cup evaporated skim milk,
    chilled
1 package (10 ounces) thawed
    frozen raspberries,
    drained, juice reserved
Water
1 envelope unflavored gelatin
¼ cup cold water
    Red food coloring (optional)
1 large angel cake
2 ripe bananas, thinly sliced
    Fresh raspberries (optional)

Pour milk into ice cube tray and freeze until ice crystals begin to form around edges. Measure reserved raspberry juice; add enough water to juice to make 1 cup. Combine gelatin with ¼ cup cold water in a saucepan. Let stand 1 minute. Heat over low heat until gelatin dissolves. Stir in reserved juice and refrigerate until cool. In mixing bowl, combine chilled gelatin mixture with milk and beat until peaks form. Add a few drops of food coloring, if desired. Mix in thawed berries. Slice angel cake horizontally into 3 layers. Frost first layer with ⅓ of raspberry mixture; top with ½ of banana slices. Repeat. Add third layer. Spread top of cake with remaining raspberry mixture. Garnish with a few fresh raspberries, if desired. Refrigerate until cold.

Makes 16 servings

	Per Serving
Calories	145
Carbohydrate (g)	33
Protein (g)	4
Total Fat (g)	0
Cholesterol (mg)	0
Sodium (mg)	49

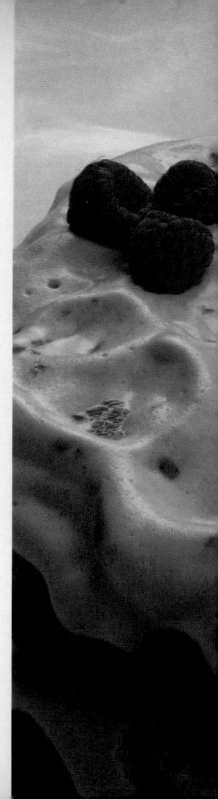

BLUSHING PEARS

1 can (16 ounces) juice-packed pear halves, drained, juice reserved
½ cup red Concord wine
½ cup unsweetened orange juice
¼ teaspoon apple pie spice

Arrange pears in 4 individual stemmed glasses. Combine pear juice with remaining ingredients in medium saucepan and bring to a boil. Lower heat and simmer, uncovered, until reduced by half. Remove from heat; let cool slightly. Pour liquid over the pears. Refrigerate until cold.

Makes 4 servings

	Per Serving
Calories	76
Carbohydrate (g)	19
Protein (g)	1
Total Fat (g)	0
Cholesterol (mg)	0
Sodium (mg)	6

RAISIN CHIP CHEWIES

½ cup diet margarine
⅓ cup packed brown sugar
1½ teaspoons vanilla
1 egg or 2 egg whites
1¼ cups sifted all-purpose flour
½ teaspoon baking soda
½ teaspoon salt
½ teaspoon ground cinnamon or apple pie spice
½ cup dark raisins

Beat together margarine, brown sugar, vanilla and egg in medium bowl. Stir flour, baking soda, salt and cinnamon together in a second bowl; add to margarine mixture. Stir in raisins and mix well. Use a measuring teaspoon to drop level spoonfuls of dough on nonstick cookie sheets. Bake in preheated 375°F oven for 8 minutes, or until cookies are golden brown. Cool on racks.

Makes about 50 cookies

	Per Cookie
Calories	30
Carbohydrate (g)	5
Protein (g)	0
Total Fat (g)	1
Cholesterol (mg)	5
Sodium (mg)	54

QUICK STRAWBERRY SAUCE

1 package (10 ounces) frozen unsweetened strawberries, thawed, drained, juice reserved
1 teaspoon cornstarch

Blend reserved juice and cornstarch in small saucepan. Heat to boiling, stirring constantly. Boil 1 minute. Remove from heat; stir in strawberries. Cool completely. (Spoon over low-fat frozen yogurt or ice milk.)

Makes about 1 cup

	Per Tablespoon
Calories	7
Carbohydrate (g)	2
Protein (g)	0
Total Fat (g)	0
Cholesterol (mg)	0
Sodium (mg)	0

Blushing Pears (top),
Raisin Chip Chewies (bottom)

RUM-PEACH SHERBET

**2 cups canned juice-packed
  sliced peaches, drained,
  juice reserved
Water
1 teaspoon lemon juice
1 envelope unflavored gelatin
2 tablespoons honey
2 teaspoons rum flavoring
  Pinch salt (optional)**

Measure reserved juice; add
water to make 1½ cups liquid.
Combine peach juice, lemon juice
and gelatin in saucepan. Let stand
1 minute for gelatin to soften.
Heat over low heat until gelatin is
dissolved. Combine all ingredients
in blender. Cover and blend on
high speed. Pour in shallow bowl
and freeze 1 hour. Remove to
mixer bowl and beat on high
speed until fluffy. Cover and
freeze until firm. Allow to soften
slightly before serving.

Makes 8 servings

	Per Serving
Calories	51
Carbohydrate (g)	12
Protein (g)	1
Total Fat (g)	0
Cholesterol (mg)	0
Sodium (mg)	4

STRAWBERRIES
À L'ORANGE

**1 pint ripe fresh strawberries
3 ounces frozen unsweetened
  orange juice concentrate,
  thawed, undiluted
1 tablespoon orange liqueur**

Wash and hull berries; leave
whole. Combine with orange juice
and liqueur in medium bowl and
mix well. Refrigerate until cold.
Spoon into 4 stemmed glasses.

Makes 4 servings

	Per Serving
Calories	67
Carbohydrate (g)	15
Protein (g)	1
Total Fat (g)	0
Cholesterol (mg)	0
Sodium (mg)	1

CHOCOLATE
PUDDING

**2 cups skim milk
2 tablespoons unsweetened
  cocoa
3 tablespoons sugar
2½ tablespoons cornstarch
¼ teaspoon salt (optional)
2 teaspoons vanilla**

Scald 1½ cups of the milk in
medium saucepan. Combine the
cocoa, sugar, cornstarch and salt
in small bowl. Blend remaining ½
cup cold milk into cocoa mixture.
Mix well. Stir into scalded milk.
Cook over very low heat, stirring
constantly, until mixture is thick.
Remove from the heat. Stir in
vanilla. Cool. Spoon into 4
individual dessert dishes and
refrigerate.

Makes 4 servings

	Per Serving
Calories	112
Carbohydrate (g)	22
Protein (g)	5
Total Fat (g)	1
Cholesterol (mg)	2
Sodium (mg)	64

FROZEN YOGURT BAKED ALASKA PIE

1 pint low-fat vanilla or
 strawberry frozen yogurt
Lean Pie Crust, baked in
 8-inch pie plate and
 cooled (see recipe in this
 chapter)
3 egg whites
 Pinch cream of tartar
6 tablespoons confectioners
 sugar
2 cups sliced strawberries or
 other fresh fruit

Soften yogurt. Spread in bottom of 8-inch baked pastry shell. Freeze solid. Beat egg whites with cream of tartar in medium bowl until soft peaks form. Gradually add sugar, beating until stiff and glossy. Remove pie from freezer. Arrange berries over yogurt. Pile meringue over berries and spread to edges of crust. Place pie on cookie sheet. Bake in preheated 500°F oven about 3 minutes or until lightly browned. Serve immediately.

Makes 8 servings

	Per Serving
Calories	146
Carbohydrate (g)	25
Protein (g)	4
Total Fat (g)	3
Cholesterol (mg)	0
Sodium (mg)	168

FRUITED BAVARIAN CREAM

1 cup evaporated skim milk
2 packages (4-serving-size)
 regular or low-calorie
 gelatin dessert mix (any
 flavor)
 Pinch salt (optional)
1½ cups boiling water
1 cup sliced fresh strawberries
 or other fruit
 Graham Cracker Crust,
 baked in 8- or 9-inch pie
 plate and cooled (see
 recipe in this chapter)

Pour evaporated skim milk into ice cube tray or metal mixing bowl. Put in freezer until ice crystals begin to form around edges. (Chill beater blades in freezer.) Dissolve gelatin mix and salt, if desired, in boiling water in small saucepan. Refrigerate until syrupy. Beat chilled skim milk at high speed until stiff, 8 to 10 minutes. Gently but thoroughly fold milk into gelatin mixture until well blended. Arrange fruit in bottom of baked crust. Cover with filling. Refrigerate several hours until set.

Hint: For Bavarian Cream Parfaits, omit pie crust. Layer fruit and filling in 6 parfait glasses. Refrigerate until set.

Makes 8 servings

	Per Serving
Calories	137
Carbohydrate (g)	26
Protein (g)	5
Total Fat (g)	2
Cholesterol (mg)	1
Sodium (mg)	164

CHOCOLATE CREAM PIE

2 envelopes unflavored gelatin
1½ cups skim milk
½ cup boiling water
¼ cup sugar
2 tablespoons unsweetened cocoa
2 teaspoons vanilla
1 pint chocolate low-fat ice milk
  Graham Cracker Crust, baked in 8- or 9-inch pie plate and cooled (see recipe in this chapter)

Combine gelatin and ⅓ cup of the skim milk in container of blender. Let stand 1 minute for gelatin to soften. Add boiling water. Cover and blend until gelatin is completely dissolved. Add remaining milk, sugar, cocoa and vanilla; cover and blend. Add ice milk; cover and blend until smooth and creamy. Refrigerate a few minutes until mixture thickens. Fill pie crust with chilled filling. Refrigerate until completely set.

Hint: For Chocolate Mini-Mousse, omit pie crust. Spoon filling into 6 dessert cups or a large bowl. Chill until set.

Makes 8 servings

Per Serving	
Calories	118
Carbohydrate (g)	17
Protein (g)	5
Total Fat (g)	4
Cholesterol (mg)	5
Sodium (mg)	103

WHIPPED MILK TOPPING

⅔ cup evaporated skim milk
3 tablespoons sugar
2 teaspoons vanilla

Pour milk into ice cube tray. Freeze until slushy. Scrape the slushy milk into chilled mixing bowl. Using chilled beaters, beat at high speed until fluffy. Add sugar and vanilla and beat until stiff. (Serve as topping on plain cake, fruit gelatin or other desserts.)

Makes 2 cups

Per Tablespoon	
Calories	10
Carbohydrate (g)	2
Protein (g)	0
Total Fat (g)	0
Cholesterol (mg)	0
Sodium (mg)	6

Chocolate Mini-Mousse (top),
Chocolate Cream Pie
with Whipped Milk Topping (bottom)

LIME OR LEMON SHERBET

1 envelope unflavored gelatin
1 cup sugar
1½ cups water
6 egg whites
1 tablespoon grated lemon or lime rind
¾ cup fresh lemon or lime juice

Combine gelatin and ½ cup of the sugar in small saucepan. Stir in water; let stand 1 minute. Heat to boiling, stirring until gelatin is completely dissolved; reserve. Beat egg whites at high speed until soft peaks form. Gradually add remaining sugar; beat until stiff. Continue to beat while adding the warm gelatin mixture in a thin steady stream. Beat in rind and juice. Pour into shallow metal trays. Freeze until slushy, stirring occasionally. Transfer to large chilled mixer bowl. With chilled beaters, quickly beat at high speed until smooth and fluffy. Return to trays; cover and freeze until firm. Allow to soften slightly before serving.

Makes 16 servings

	Per Serving
Calories	58
Carbohydrate (g)	13
Protein (g)	2
Total Fat (g)	0
Cholesterol (mg)	0
Sodium (mg)	22

STRAWBERRY ICE MILK

2 teaspoons unflavored gelatin
1 cup cold water
¾ cup instant dry nonfat milk crystals
1½ cups skim milk
⅔ cup sugar
2 teaspoons vanilla
1 tablespoon lemon juice
1 cup fresh or frozen unsweetened strawberries, mashed or pureed

Soften gelatin in ½ cup of the cold water in small cup. Combine ¼ cup of milk crystals with skim milk in a saucepan; heat over low heat. Add gelatin mixture and heat until dissolved. Add ½ cup of the sugar, stirring until dissolved. Stir in vanilla. Refrigerate until slightly thickened. Beat remaining ½ cup milk crystals and ½ cup of cold water until it begins to thicken slightly. Add lemon juice and remaining sugar and beat 5 minutes or until consistency of whipped cream. Fold in chilled gelatin mixture. Spoon into refrigerator trays. Freeze until edges are set. Remove to mixer bowl and beat on high speed until fluffy. Cover and freeze until firm. Allow to soften slightly before serving.

Hints: For Banana Ice Milk, substitute 2 very ripe bananas, mashed, for strawberries.

For Chocolate Ice Milk, omit strawberries. Add 3 tablespoons unsweetened cocoa and 3 additional tablespoons sugar when adding the ½ cup sugar to the warm milk mixture.

Makes 8 servings

	Per Serving
Calories	115
Carbohydrate (g)	24
Protein (g)	4
Total Fat (g)	0
Cholesterol (mg)	2
Sodium (mg)	60

Strawberry Ice Milk (top),
Lime Sherbet (bottom)

YOGURT PEACH QUICHE

Lean Pie Crust (see recipe in this chapter)
2½ cups thinly sliced, pared fresh or juice-packed canned peaches, drained
½ cup liquid egg substitute
1 cup low-fat vanilla yogurt
¼ cup sugar
Ground cinnamon

Line 8-inch nonstick pie pan with Lean Pie Crust. Add peaches in single layer. Combine egg substitute, yogurt and sugar in medium bowl. Mix well; pour over peaches. Sprinkle with cinnamon. Bake in preheated 450°F oven for 15 minutes. Reduce heat to 325°F and bake 30 minutes longer, or until custard is set.

Hint: For Yogurt Peach Custard, omit pie shell; layer fruit and filling in 6 ovenproof custard cups. Bake in a preheated 350°F oven until set, 30 to 40 minutes.

Makes 8 servings

	Per Serving
Calories	132
Carbohydrate (g)	22
Protein (g)	4
Total Fat (g)	3
Cholesterol (mg)	1
Sodium (mg)	200

BLUEBERRY TOPPING

1 pint fresh or frozen unsweetened blueberries
2 tablespoons sugar
1 teaspoon cornstarch
¼ teaspoon ground cinnamon

Combine all ingredients in small saucepan. Cook and stir 2 minutes over low heat. Cool completely.

Makes about 1½ cups

	Per Tablespoon
Calories	11
Carbohydrate (g)	3
Protein (g)	0
Total Fat (g)	0
Cholesterol (mg)	0
Sodium (mg)	1

LEAN PIE CRUST

½ cup sifted all-purpose flour
¼ teaspoon salt
¼ teaspoon baking powder
¼ cup diet margarine, softened

Stir together flour, salt and baking powder in a bowl. Cut in margarine with fork or pastry blender and continue mixing until no pastry sticks to the sides of the bowl. Shape into a ball. Wrap and refrigerate for 1 hour or more. Roll dough out on floured board and fit into pie plate. If prebaking, heat oven to 425°F and bake about 12 minutes, until golden. This recipe makes single crust to line an 8- or 9-inch pie plate. For a 2-crust pie, double the recipe.

Makes 8 servings

	Per Serving
Calories	51
Carbohydrate (g)	6
Protein (g)	1
Total Fat (g)	3
Cholesterol (mg)	0
Sodium (mg)	149

STRAWBERRY-APPLE FIZZ

3 ounces unsweetened frozen
  apple juice concentrate,
  thawed, undiluted
1 envelope unflavored gelatin
1 cup boiling water
1½ cups frozen whole
  unsweetened strawberries,
  not thawed

Put apple juice in blender
container and sprinkle on gelatin.
Let stand 1 minute until gelatin
softens; then add boiling water.
Cover and blend until gelatin
granules are dissolved. Add frozen
berries. Cover and blend until
liquefied. Pour into 4 glass dessert
cups and chill until set. (Fizz
separates into layers.) For variety
use other fruits and juices except
pineapple.

Makes 4 servings

Per Serving	
Calories	61
Carbohydrate (g)	14
Protein (g)	2
Total Fat (g)	0
Cholesterol (mg)	0
Sodium (mg)	8

BANANA YOGURT PIE

1 envelope unflavored gelatin
2 tablespoons cold water
½ cup boiling water
3 tablespoons sugar
1½ cups low-fat vanilla yogurt
  Graham Cracker Crust,
  baked in 8- or 9-inch pie
  plate and cooled (see
  recipe in this chapter)
2 small bananas, thinly sliced
  Ground cinnamon

Combine gelatin and cold water
in blender container. Let stand 1
minute for gelatin to soften. Add
boiling water and sugar; cover and
blend until gelatin is completely
dissolved. Add yogurt; cover and
blend. Refrigerate mixture 15
minutes. Spread half of chilled
filling in pie crust; cover with layer
of banana slices. Top with
remaining filling and sprinkle with
cinnamon. Refrigerate until set.

Makes 8 servings

Per Serving	
Calories	97
Carbohydrate (g)	16
Protein (g)	3
Total Fat (g)	3
Cholesterol (mg)	2
Sodium (mg)	81

REFRIGERATOR CHEESECAKE

Graham Cracker Crust (see recipe in this chapter)
2 envelopes unflavored gelatin
½ cup cold water
2 eggs, separated
¾ cup skim milk
4 tablespoons sugar
1 cup low-fat cottage cheese
2 teaspoons fresh lemon juice
1 teaspoon grated lemon rind
2 teaspoons vanilla
4 tablespoons honey
½ cup nonfat instant dry milk crystals
½ cup ice-cold water

Prepare unbaked Graham Cracker Crust in 8-inch springform pan. Refrigerate. Sprinkle gelatin over ½ cup of cold water in large bowl to soften. Beat egg yolks in top of double boiler until fluffy. Add skim milk and sugar. Place over hot water. Cook, stirring constantly, until thick. Add gelatin mixture; stir until dissolved. Remove from heat and pour into blender. Add cheese, lemon juice, rind, vanilla and honey. Cover and blend until smooth. Refrigerate until slightly thickened. Beat egg whites in small bowl until stiff but not dry. In another bowl, beat nonfat dry milk and ½ cup ice-cold water until creamy. Gently but thoroughly fold beaten egg whites into cheese mixture. Gently fold in the whipped milk mixture. Spoon cheesecake mixture into prepared crust. Refrigerate several hours until set.

Makes 12 servings

	Per Serving
Calories	99
Carbohydrate (g)	13
Protein (g)	6
Total Fat (g)	3
Cholesterol (mg)	47
Sodium (mg)	148

RAW FRUIT GLAZE FOR CHEESECAKE OR PIE

1 tablespoon cornstarch
1 cup unsweetened peach juice or other unsweetened fruit juice
Sugar to taste (optional)
2 cups sliced fresh peaches or other sliced fruit or whole berries

Blend cornstarch with juice in small saucepan. Cook over low heat, stirring constantly, until clear and thickened. Add sugar; stir until sugar is dissolved. Set aside to cool. Arrange peach slices on top of cheesecake or pie. Spoon sauce over fruit.

Makes 12 servings

	Per Serving
Calories	26
Carbohydrate (g)	7
Protein (g)	0
Total Fat (g)	0
Cholesterol (mg)	0
Sodium (mg)	2

Refrigerator Cheesecake with Raw Fruit Glaze

NECTAR WHIP

2 envelopes unflavored gelatin
½ cup cold water
¼ cup honey
1 can (12 ounces)
    unsweetened peach or
    apricot nectar
2 teaspoons lemon juice
3 egg whites

Combine gelatin and water in a saucepan. Wait 1 minute until gelatin softens; then cook over low heat, stirring constantly, until gelatin dissolves. Remove from heat. Stir in honey, peach nectar and lemon juice. Refrigerate, stirring occasionally, until mixture is syrupy-thick. Add egg whites to gelatin. Beat at high speed with electric mixer until light and fluffy. Refrigerate until firm.

Makes 8 servings

Per Serving	
Calories	70
Carbohydrate (g)	15
Protein (g)	3
Total Fat (g)	0
Cholesterol (mg)	0
Sodium (mg)	24

CHILLED ORANGE SOUFFLÉ

1 envelope unflavored gelatin
½ cup sugar
1 cup water
1 can (6 ounces) frozen
    unsweetened orange juice
    concentrate, undiluted,
    thawed
½ cup ice water
½ cup instant nonfat dry milk
    crystals

2 tablespoons lemon juice
Cantaloupe, green grapes,
    blueberries or other fresh
    fruit (optional)

Mix together unflavored gelatin and ¼ cup of the sugar in saucepan; stir in 1 cup water. Heat over low heat, stirring constantly, until gelatin is dissolved. Remove from heat; stir in orange juice concentrate. Refrigerate, stirring occasionally, until mixture is the consistency of unbeaten egg white. While mixture is chilling, pour ½ cup ice water into a mixing bowl; add nonfat dry milk crystals. Beat until soft peaks form, 3 to 4 minutes. Add lemon juice. Continue beating until firm peaks form, 3 to 4 minutes longer. Gradually add remaining ¼ cup sugar. Fold in gelatin mixture. Turn into serving bowl; refrigerate until firm. Garnish with fresh fruit, if desired.

Makes 8 servings

Per Serving	
Calories	101
Carbohydrate (g)	23
Protein (g)	3
Total Fat (g)	0
Cholesterol (mg)	1
Sodium (mg)	26

Chilled Orange Soufflé

GRAHAM CRACKER CRUST

¾ cup plain graham cracker crumbs
3 tablespoons diet margarine, softened

Mix crumbs and margarine with fork in a bowl until thoroughly blended. Press mixture firmly and evenly onto bottom and sides of nonstick 8- or 9-inch pie plate for pie crust or 8-inch springform pan for cheesecake crust. For pie crust, bake in a preheated 400°F oven 5 minutes. Cool before filling. For cheesecake, refrigerate unbaked crust about 45 minutes before filling.

Makes 8 servings

	Per Serving
Calories	54
Carbohydrate (g)	7
Protein (g)	1
Total Fat (g)	3
Cholesterol (mg)	0
Sodium (mg)	114

TANGY FRUIT TOPPING

4 ounces low-fat cream cheese, softened
¾ cup low-fat plain yogurt
¼ cup unsweetened frozen pineapple or orange juice concentrate, thawed, undiluted
1 teaspoon grated orange or lemon rind (optional)

Combine ingredients in medium bowl and beat until fluffy. (Serve on fresh fruit.)

Makes 1¼ cups

	Per Tablespoon
Calories	16
Carbohydrate (g)	2
Protein (g)	1
Total Fat (g)	0
Cholesterol (mg)	1
Sodium (mg)	19

COCOA KISSES

3 egg whites
½ teaspoon cream of tartar
1 cup sugar
2 tablespoons unsweetened cocoa

Beat egg whites in medium bowl until foamy. Add cream of tartar; beat until soft peaks form. Gradually beat in sugar, a few tablespoons at a time. Beat until stiff. Fold in cocoa. Drop batter by level teaspoonsful on nonstick cookie sheets which have been sprayed with cooking spray. Bake in preheated 275°F oven 18 to 20 minutes. Cool completely before removing from pans. Store in a very dry place.

Makes about 8 dozen

	Per Serving
Calories	9
Carbohydrate (g)	2
Protein (g)	0
Total Fat (g)	0
Cholesterol (mg)	0
Sodium (mg)	2